JES
ESSENTIAL R

The Revd Canon Anthony Duncan
is Vicar of Warkworth,
Northumberland, and an Honorary
Canon of Newcastle Cathedral. He is
the author of several books on
Christian spirituality, including
The Whole Christ (SPCK, 1968),
The Christ, Psychotherapy and Magic
(Allen and Unwin, 1969),
The Priesthood of Man (Bles, 1973),
and *The Fourth Dimension* (Mowbray,
1975). He lectures extensively and is an
experienced Retreat Conductor. Canon
Duncan is married with three grown-up
children.

JESUS
ESSENTIAL READINGS

ANTHONY DUNCAN

First published 1986

British Library
Cataloguing in Publication Data
Duncan, Anthony D.
Jesus: essential readings
1. Jesus Christ — Teaching
I. Title
232.9'54   BS2415.A2
ISBN 0-85030-555-1
ISBN 0-85030-395-8 Pbk

Crucible is an imprint of
The Aquarian Press,
part of the Thorsons Publishing Group

Printed and bound in Great Britain

CONTENTS

ACKNOWLEDGEMENTS

I AM indebted to Nashdom Abbey (The Pershore and Nashdom Trust Ltd) for permission to make use of the late Dom Robert Petitpierre's *The Poems of Jesus*; to SCM Press Ltd for permission to quote from A. M. Hunter's *The Work and Words of Jesus*; to Fontana Paperbacks for permission to quote from Victor White's *God and the Unconscious*; to Oxford University Press for permission to quote from *The Oxford Dictitionary of the Christian Church*; to Doubleday & Company Inc. for permission to quote from Grant and Freedman's *The Secret Sayings of Jesus*; to Macmillan Accounts and Administration Ltd for permission to quote from William Temple's *Readings in St John's Gospel*; and to Darton, Longman & Todd Ltd for permission to quote from Rabbi Lionel Blue's *To Heaven With Scribes and Pharisees*.

In addition, I am grateful to the following for their permission to make use of texts in which they hold copyright: E. J. Brill, Leiden, the Netherlands, and Harper and Row, Publishers Inc., for verses from The Gospel of Thomas from *The Nag Hammadi Library, in English*, translated by Members of the Coptic Gnostic Library Project of the Institute of Antiquity and Christianity, James M. Robinson, Director (copyright © E. J. Brill 1978); the National Council of the Churches of Christ in the USA for use of the Revised Standard Version text; and the Westminster Press, Philadelphia, Pennsylvania, for material from *The Other Gospels* by Ron Cameron.

SELECT BIBLIOGRAPHY

GOSPELS/SAYINGS OF JESUS

C. H. Dodd, *The Fourth Gospel* (Cambridge, 1953).

F. C. Grant, *The Gospels, Their Origin and Their Growth* (Faber, 1957).

A. M. Hunter, *The Work and Words of Jesus* (SCM, 1950).

R. H. Lightfoot, *St John's Gospel* (Oxford, 1960).

R. Petitpierre, *The Poems of Jesus* (Faith Press, 1965).

J. H. Ropes, *The Synoptic Gospels* (Oxford, 1934).

W. Temple, *Readings in St John's Gospel* (Macmillan, 1945).

J. M. Thompson, *The Synoptic Gospels* (Oxford, 1910).

APOCRYPHA

R. Cameron, *The Other Gospels* (Lutterworth, 1983).

Grant and Freedman, *The Secret Sayings of Jesus* (Fontana, 1960).

M. R. James, *The Apocryphal New Testament* (Oxford, 1924).

E. Pagels, *The Gnostic Gospels* (Penguin, 1979).

COMMENTARIES

St Matthew's Gospel
   W. Barclay (2 vols., St Andrews, 1956).
   J. Fenton (Penguin, 1977).

St Mark's Gospel
   W. Barclay (St Andrews, 1954).
   D. E. Nineham (Penguin, 1956).

St Luke's Gospel
   W. Barclay (St Andrews, 1953).
   G. B. Caird (Penguin, 1971).

St John's Gospel
   W. Barclay (2 vols., St Andrews, 1955).
   John Marsh (Penguin, 1971).

1

THE MAN HIMSELF

Who was Jesus?

WE shall be studying the reported sayings of a young man who was almost certainly known to his village contemporaries as Joshua bar Joseph. We know remarkably little about him. The name by which he is usually known, Jesus, is the Greek form of his Hebrew name, rather as Iain is the Gaelic form of the English John. The name Joshua means 'God saves' and it was a common enough name among young Jews. The word 'Christ', commonly added to the name Jesus, is an anglicized version of the Greek *Christus*. This in turn is the Greek for the Hebrew word *Messiah,* which literally means 'anointed'. In the early Old Testament the King was known as 'the Lord's anointed', the one consecrated by God to rule over His people. By the first century AD the term had become popularly identified with a long-hoped-for deliverer, sent by God, who would deliver His people out of their centuries-long subservience to foreign powers and occupying armies and establish justice and righteousness on earth—with, it was often hoped, the Jews as 'top nation'!

Our sources of information

Outside the pages of the New Testament there is very little to find about Jesus. There are a few references in the Jewish *Talmud,* but they are mostly late in date, slanderous, and pretty well worthless: 'The sum of what they say is that Jesus practised sorcery, ridiculed the wise men, led the people astray and was hanged on the eve of the Passover. His disciples, five in number, cured sick people in their Master's name. What these references do prove is that there is no reason to doubt the existence of Jesus, as a few cranks still do. Men, as a rule, do not vehemently slander myths.' [1]

Three Latin writers refer to Jesus. Pliny, governor of Bithinia, wrote to the Emperor Trajan in about AD 112, reporting that the Christians

[1] A. M. Hunter, *The Work and Words of Jesus* (SCM, 1950), p. 15.

were wont 'on a fixed day to assemble before daylight and sing by turns a hymn to Christ as a god'. About three years later, Tacitus, in his *Annals*, tells how the great fire in Rome was blamed on the Christians and explains: 'Christ, from whom they derive their name, was put to death in the reign of Tiberius by the procurator Pontius Pilate.' A contemporary of Tacitus, Suetonius, records that the Emperor Claudius 'banished the Jews from Rome where they made a constant rioting at the instigation of Chrestus'. Clearly Suetonius thought that Jesus had been present as a troublemaker at the time, for 'Chrestus' is almost certainly a corruption of *Christus.*

The only other source of information is the Jewish historian Josephus, who makes mention of Jesus twice in his *Antiquities.* One passage records the stoning to death of 'James, the brother of Jesus who was called the Christ'. The second passage is slightly suspect, for it reads: 'Jesus, a wise man, if indeed we should call him a man, for he was a doer of miracles and a master of men who receive the truth with joy . . . He was the Christ.' Why suspect? Because Josephus was a Jew and there is no reason to suppose that he ever became a Christian believer. Scepticism will suspect here a later interpolation by a Christian hand, but there is no way of proving this.

The New Testament

Secular sources having helped us very little, we are now driven back upon the religious texts. It will be necessary for us to acquaint ourselves with what they are and how they assumed their present form. Out of a large number of Christian writings, and an equally large number of quasi-Christian writings, the present canon of Holy Scripture came to command general acceptance and to be recognized as authoritative.

The word *canon* is the Greek for 'measuring rod'. The Four Gospels, together with the Epistles (letters) of St Paul, had come to be accepted as reliable and authoritative by about AD 130, though scholars differ to a remarkable degree about such matters as the dates of the various books. The remaining books won gradual acceptance until by about the time of St Athanasius (*c.*369) the New Testament as we have it now was generally accepted as inspired Scripture.

The Church has been nothing if not cautious, but the *character* of Jesus, the Christ, and of his message, as recorded in the canonical books is not only consistent, but consistent with the Risen Christ as he is known by the Church, that is to say, by the great mass of succeeding generations of Christian believers, in her life and in her liturgy. Of the non-canonical books, or the Apocryphal New Testament as it is usually known, we shall have something to say later on. But now we must turn our attention to the four Gospels, attributed to the Saints Matthew, Mark, Luke, and John.

At this stage it must be said that the last century and a half has seen an academic assault upon these four books which is probably unparalleled in any other learned discipline. It would not be hard for an outside observer to interpret this as an almost frantic effort to dissect, discredit, reject, and destroy, particularly in recent decades. It must be said that this has not been the intention and a very great deal of this scholarship has been in the highest degree enlightening, some of it less so. As the various academic tides have ebbed and flowed about this thing or that, some learned men have doubted if any of the actual words of Jesus can be identified with certainty, while others have taken— and still take—every place on the spectrum from extreme radicalism to equally extreme conservatism. From an academic point of view the subject might have all the appearance of a minefield, but we shall cross it with something like abandon because the journey must be made and this is the only way to make it for we are not, in this work, primarily engaged in an academic exercise.

The Four Gospels

The word *gospel* is derived from the Old English *godspel*, which translated the Greek *evaggalion* meaning 'good news'. To Christian believers the Good News is Jesus himself rather than anything he is reported as saying. In a narrower sense the word Gospel refers to the written accounts of his life, work, and words. These things cannot be separated as far as the Christian Church is concerned for it is *who he is* that is of the prime importance. What he did is a consequence of who he is, and so is what he said also a consequence of who he is. His words are of secondary importance, however important they are in themselves.

Our present task, that of anthologizing the reported words of Jesus, is rarely undertaken. Indeed it is only in such works as the apocryphal Gospel of Thomas, a late and suspiciously 'esoteric' compilation, that we find the words attributed to Jesus isolated from his life and works. It is necessary, therefore, that we are quite clear what we are about in this present undertaking.

Out of the intense academic debate has emerged a number of broadly accepted conclusions upon which we may rely with a fair confidence. They will help us to consider such matters as the authorship of the various Gospels, possible dates of compilation, the sources used, and the general drift of presentation. It is worth mentioning that the letters written by St Paul to the various Christian congregations are possibly a full decade earlier in date than the earliest of the four Gospels and date from the middle to late fifties of the first century.

It is also important to remember that the Gospels were not compiled in a vacuum. 'The beginning of the good news of Jesus Christ, the Son of God' is the very first sentence in Mark. St John is clear that 'these are written that you may believe that Jesus is the Christ, the Son of God, and that believing you may have life in his name'. The Gospels are a proclamation of Good News by men who were utterly committed to it. Their belief was total. Nobody else would have bothered!

The Synoptic Gospels

The first three Gospels, those attributed to Matthew, Mark, and Luke, are known as the Synoptic Gospels because they give a common synopsis, or brief general description, of the life and work of Jesus. With the possible exception of Mark they are compiled from a variety of already existing sources. Matthew and Luke reproduce the text of Mark almost in its entirety, with some editing and rephrasing, as the narrative framework for their much longer works. This suggests that Mark is the earliest of the three, and there is evidence to suggest that Mark, having been an early travelling companion of St Paul, was later closely associated with St Peter and recorded what he had learned from him. But Mark's connection with Jesus might have been closer still, for there is a strong tradition that the Last Supper took place in his mother's house in Jerusalem, Mark being a teenager at the time. The brief reference in Mark to a young man narrowly escaping arrest with Jesus is generally regarded as autobiographical.

Mark—there is no reason to doubt his authorship—presents a stark and vivid portrait of Jesus. It is almost an extended Passion narrative, with Jesus portrayed throughout as being in an awful and deepening isolation. Mark's supreme concern is with *who Jesus is*. The works, as recorded, reflect this and it is surprising how relatively few of his words are recorded, by comparison with the other Gospel writers.

Sources of the Sayings of Jesus

Collections of the sayings of Jesus appear to have been in existence before any of the Gospels appeared in their present form. There is a broad consensus among scholars that at least three were extant, and these have been identified under the letters 'Q', 'L', and 'M'.

The main source, thought to have been in existence by about AD 50, is known by the letter 'Q' (from *Quelle*, German for Source) and comprises that material which is common to both Luke and Matthew, but which is not found in Mark. It is not difficult to reconstruct and it adds up to some 250 verses. Where there are variations between the Lukan and Matthean treatment of the same material, the former suggests itself as the more primitive and the Lukan sequence of 'Q' material the more convincing. We can therefore reconstruct it in four parts:

> Jesus and John the Baptist
> Jesus and his disciples
> Jesus and his opponents
> Jesus and the future. [2]

Two other sources remain. The first is that peculiar to Luke which we call 'L'. The exclusively Lukan material contains both narrative and teaching. From a quite separate source came the stories, in the first two chapters, concerning the birth of Jesus. These latter come from what is probably an Aramaic original and give all the appearance of a last-minute insertion into an already completed Gospel. (The 'joins' are easily detected in the narrative.) These are not reckoned among the 'L' material, which is divisible into eight sections:

John and Jesus	Rejection at Nazareth
Mighty Works	Various Lessons
Various Warnings	Parables of the lost
Parables of responsibility	Events at Jerusalem

It has been suggested that these represent an oral tradition, gathered by St Luke while at Caesarea during the period of St Paul's detention there, c.AD 57-59. There exist traditions which connect the Birth stories with the Mother of Jesus with whom, according to tradition, St Luke was acquainted. Nothing certain can be said of this. There is no reason to doubt the actual authorship of the Gospel as we have it, nor need we doubt that it represents the first volume of a two-volume work of which the Acts of the Apostles is the second.

The source known as 'M' is rather different. Eusebius, a third-

[2] ibid., p. 131.

century historian, quotes a garbled reference by one Papias (d.130) to Matthew as having 'composed the oracles in Hebrew'. It must be said that there is no certainty at all concerning the authorship of the Gospel attributed to Matthew: 'What is certain is that it represents a distinct style of tradition with a clear Jewish tincture. Its respect for law, coupled with its hatred of the lawyers, its Palestinian Jewish atmosphere . . . and its strong Church interest suggest that it emanated from the Churches of Judea, which were centred in the Jerusalem Mother Church, and that it [that is to say, the 'M' source] belongs to the years just before the Fall of Jerusalem [AD 70].'[3]

'M' can be said to consist of about a dozen proof-texts from the Old Testament (are these, perhaps, the 'oracles' referred to by Papias?), a dozen assorted narratives, some of which suggest Jerusalem gossip, and a very considerable collection of sayings and parables. The arrangement of the material is very much more contrived than in Luke. It is arranged in discourses, as if for coherent reading in church. In some respects Matthew has to be treated with more caution than Mark and Luke as some scholars have detected hints of possible adulteration from the Jewish Christian interest.

To summarize, therefore, we may recognize the Synoptic Gospels as being made up essentially as follows:

Mark: Whatever his sources, we will regard this as an
           original text.
Luke: Mark + 'Q' + 'L' + Birth Stories.
Matthew: Mark + 'Q' + 'M'.

We must now attend to a very different document, a veritable happy-hunting-ground for the contentious scholar: the Gospel according to St John.

The Fourth Gospel

At first sight, the Gospel according to St John appears to be startlingly different from the Synoptics. Its authorship is a matter of considerable debate but there is a wide measure of assent to William Temple's opinion: 'I regard as self-condemned any theory which fails to find a very close connection between the Gospel and John the son of Zebedee.'[4]

[3] ibid., p. 147.
[4] William Temple, *Readings in St John's Gospel* (Macmillan, 1938), p. x.

Commenting on evidence that a certain John the Elder, a disciple of John the Apostle, may have been the actual author, Temple concludes: 'The view which now seems to do fullest justice to the evidence is that the writer—the Evangelist—was John the Elder, who was an intimate disciple of John the Apostle; that he records the teaching of that Apostle with great fidelity; that the Apostle is the "Witness" to whom reference is sometimes made, and is also the "disciple whom Jesus loved". It may be that the Apostle actually dictated to the Elder parts of what now constitutes the Gospel; I incline to think so, but parts are the Elder's own recollections of the Apostle's teaching and parts are his own comment . . . It is not possible to say which sections of the Gospel come direct from the Apostle; but I am sure that we are nearer the truth in maximising than in minimising these.'[5]

Historical reliability

It is sometimes argued that the Fourth Gospel cannot be reconciled with the Synoptics in respect of the sequence of events. The Synoptics, however, make no attempt to do more than their common, minimal, Markan framework provides for, and this essentially presents the story of the Passion of Jesus. Indeed they provide no chronology at all, apart from that last week, and their narrative is unintelligible unless something very like the Johannine story is accepted. John and the Synoptics differ as to the actual day of the Crucifixion, but the Johannine version, pinpointing the Day of Preparation as the day of the crucifixion, is by far the more credible and is, indeed, generally accepted.

The picture of Jesus

It is sometimes argued that 'a different Jesus' is portrayed by the Fourth Gospel. This is not the case. Temple contends 'that there is no incompatibility between the Synoptic and Johannine portraits, because the Synoptic portrait is substantially Johannine'.[6]

The teaching of Jesus

To a considerable degree the marked differences between the teaching of Jesus as recorded in the Synoptics and that recorded in St John can be accounted for by the fact that the Synoptics record sayings delivered to 'the multitude' or to local religious leaders in Galilee. The Fourth Gospel records intimate converse with the disciples, or controversy with

[5] ibid., p. xxi.
[6] ibid., p. xxvi.

the far more sophisticated religious leaders in Jerusalem, whose context was the Temple rather than the local synagogue.

Are the Johannine sayings attributed to Jesus the *ipissima verba* of Jesus, or are they reconstructions by the Evangelist? Scholarly debate waxes furious on this point but the answer is, almost certainly, both. Temple reminds us that 'the convention of historical writing in the ancient world approved the attribution to leading personages of speeches expressing what is known to be their view in a form which is due to the historian. In such compositions key-phrases actually spoken would naturally be recorded.'[7] Temple concludes that 'each conversation or discourse contained in the Gospel actually took place. But it is so reported as to convey, not only the sounds uttered or the meaning then apprehended, but the meaning which, always there, has been disclosed by lifelong meditation.'[8] In some cases conversations, such as the one with the woman at the well in Samaria, are reported without comments; in others, such as, possibly, that with Nicodemus, overheard by the Apostle John and thus part of his own experience, reporting passes over into comment. But, Temple warns, 'we are wise to regard all that we can as utterance of the Lord in the sense described, and to put the point of transition to comment on the part of either the Beloved Disciple (the Witness) or the Evangelist as late in the text as possible'.[9]

A note of caution, however, is sounded by the late Dom Robert Petitpierre in his book, *Poems of Jesus:* 'It is the fashion to regard the sayings in John as having been interpreted by the mind of the evangelist. My own attempt to find patterns of poetry in the Johannine sayings leads me to think that such a judgement needs careful revision. At any rate, we find in the long discourses in John a considerable number of small units of poetry whose pattern is remarkably similar to that we find in the other Gospels.'[10] This mention of poetry attributable to Jesus leads us to consider the style of his teaching and its presentation.

The style of Jesus' teaching

In the days before the written word became generally available, when books had a mystique attached to them which we can no longer imagine, and when the spoken word was almost the sole means of teaching and mass communication, it was essential for a teacher so to present

[7] ibid., p. xvii.
[8] ibid., p. xviii.
[9] ibid., p. xix.
[10] Dom Robert Petitpierre OSB, *Poems of Jesus* (Faith Press, 1965), p. 93.

his teachings that they would be clearly grasped and remembered. This required of a teacher that he be both a poet and storyteller, and there can be little doubt that Jesus was exceedingly accomplished in both media. Most of all, perhaps, he was a poet.

The conventions of Hebrew poetry required *ideas* to rhyme, not just word-endings. Thus Hebrew poetry survives translation essentially intact. All the books of the New Testament were written in that Greek which was the *lingua franca* of the Eastern Roman Empire. Doubtless Jesus was bilingual to some degree, but his teachings were given in his native Aramaic and everything that is recorded as being his words is a translation from an Aramaic original. Such is the nature of Hebrew poetry, however, that its poetic form remains essentially intact. Hebrew poetry relied on the repetition of stressed syllables in each line (rhythm) and on the repetition of sounds (rhyme); but it is the rhyming of ideas, or, more correctly, *parallelism*, which makes it possible for us to identify what we may quite reasonably describe as the 'Poems of Jesus'. In his book bearing that name, Petitpierre identified almost two hundred poetically constructed teachings in the Gospels.

The *Parables*, the vivid similitudes drawn from nature or from human affairs, are well known. They provoke the hearers to go away and think, and to find various levels of meaning and of application. Parable was a common teaching form and by no means exclusive to Jesus. His mastery of the form is nevertheless remarkable. Poetry, likewise, has the quality of being able to give utterance to the 'unsayable', and to convey meaning at many different levels. The frequent challenge uttered by Jesus to his hearers, 'He who has ears, let him hear', is a call for a thoughtful and creative response to an utterance that demands that kind of 'homework'. Never does Jesus descend to the level of formal instruction in flat prose. Had he done so, and in such a context as first-century Palestine, his words would have been instantly forgotten and their entire meaning lost!

The date of the Gospel records

Scholars are in considerable dispute over the question of dating the books of the New Testament, and in particular the Gospels. A widely-held view until recently was that the sources behind the Gospels as we have them might have been compiled by, say, AD 50, St Mark's Gospel, the first written, appearing in the mid-60s, shortly after the martyrdom of Peter and Paul. The Gospels according to Matthew and Luke may have come a decade or so later, and that of St John in the

80s of the first century. More recent scholarship tends to see the Gospels in their present form appearing as late as the middle of the second century, some now advancing St John's Gospel as the first to be completed. There was certainly a considerable degree of literary activity at that time and many of the apocryphal gospels can be traced to about that period.

A very different view, also of recent scholarship, would see the New Testament as we have it completed by the end of the 60s of the first century. The point is made that no clear reference is to be found to the Fall of Jerusalem, or of the destruction of the Temple in AD 70, following a Jewish insurrection. It is inconceivable, so it is argued, that such an event would not have been mentioned had it happened before the accounts were completed.

The faith of the early Church

The Gospel records were compiled within the context of an intense belief, and if the question be then asked what that belief was in its earliest and most primitive form, a passage in one of St Paul's Letters, written in the early 50s, gives us the primitive *Kerygma* or proclamation of the Faith. Writing to the congregation in the city of Corinth, he says: 'I delivered to you as of first importance what I also received; that Christ died for our sins in accordance with the scriptures, that he was buried, that he was raised on the third day in accordance with the scriptures, and that he appeared to Cephas [St Peter], then to the twelve [his intimate followers]. Then he appeared to more than five hundred brethren at one time, most of whom are still alive, though some have fallen asleep. Then he appeared to James, then to all the apostles. Last of all, as to one untimely born, he appeared also to me.' The phrase 'in accordance with the scriptures' means in complete congruity with the Theism as developed and enshrined in the Old Testament.

It was therefore *the experience of Jesus* by the early Christians that brought the books of the New Testament into being. It was the continuing experience of the same Jesus by the Christian community (the Church) in her life, in her liturgy, in her fellowship, and in her prayers both corporate and private—and not least in her sufferings—which recognized *a character and an authority* in some of the many written works that was not present in others. Thus the *canon* of the New Testament was established.

The Apocryphal New Testament

The Fourth Gospel ends with an engaging and somewhat tantalizing remark: 'There are also many things which Jesus did; were every one of them to be written, I suppose that the world itself could not contain the books that would be written.' St Luke begins by saying: 'Many have undertaken to compile a narrative of the things which have been accomplished among us, just as they were delivered to us by those who from the beginning were eyewitnesses and ministers of the word.' We wonder who the 'many' are, and what the 'other things' were that Jesus did. What more might there be to find out about the work and words of Jesus?

We learn a certain amount from the other New Testament books, but it is to the apocryphal gospels that we are tempted to turn lest, perhaps, something important has been omitted from the more conventional sources.

The epithet *aprocryphal* does not of itself imply inaccuracy, unauthenticity, or unorthodoxy, and many such gospels exist, and 'it is possible that in a few places some of these embody trustworthy oral traditions, e.g. the *Gospel According to the Hebrews* and that *According to the Egyptians*. Others such as the Gospels of *Marcion*, of *the Twelve Apostles,* of *Thomas* and of *Philip* were intended to support heretical and especially Gnostic views. A third group set out to satisfy the popular curiosity with tales of the Childhood of Christ, his Passion and his post-Resurrection life; their contents were often patently garrulous and their ideas not infrequently immoral . . . Most of these works lie between the late 1st and early 3rd centuries.'[11]

It is hard to read these works without a sense of disappointment, and it is not hard to see how they failed to win acceptance by more than handfuls of Christians, many of whom were on the eccentric fringes of Christian belief. Nevertheless, these documents exist and occasional gems may be found buried in some of them.

The Resurrection

A unique feature of the whole *ambience* of the Gospels is that they bear witness to Christian belief that Jesus rose from the dead. This belief is in fact the main motive for this compilation. In an anthology of sayings this state of affairs introduces a wholly unique feature in that some of the sayings and teachings of Jesus are presented as having

---

[11] *Oxford Dictionary of the Christian Church,* 'Apocryphal New Testament'.

been uttered, not merely *post mortem* but *post-Resurrection*. And yet it is, we are assured, the same Jesus who is talking to us: 'It is I myself; handle me and see; for a spirit has not flesh and bones as you see I have.' St Luke, recording the bewilderment of the disciples, confronted with the Jesus whom they had seen die, tells us: 'While they still disbelieved for joy, and wondered, he said to them, "Have you anything here to eat?" They gave him a piece of broiled fish, and he took it and ate before them.' A quite unique claim is being made here. In the light of it we shall have difficulty in arbitrarily excluding the words of the Risen Jesus to Paul, or to John on the island of Patmos. Where, we may ask, does it end?

In conclusion

We shall be encountering the words—the reported words—of a young man of whom, historically, remarkably little is known, who never wrote down a word for posterity, and who was dishonestly 'got rid of' by the authorities on a trumped-up charge, as a politico-religious nuisance, in his mid-thirties. And all of that a very long time ago.

The *experience of Jesus*, however, caused his followers to claim what they have continued to claim for almost two thousand years, namely: 'God was in Christ reconciling the world to himself.'

THE ANTHOLOGY

PART 1

From New Testament Sources

2

THE PRESENTION

THE material used in this part of the anthology is drawn from the New Testament and is presented under ten general headings, each with a brief introductory essay. Any selection of headings must be, to a considerable degree, arbitrary, and much of the material could be assembled under different headings. Jesus did not indulge in 'systematic theology', nor did he tidily arrange his teaching under headings. I have avoided, where possible, words which have become theological technical terms, like 'salvation', 'redemption', and so forth, and in the introductory essays I have confined myself as far as possible to broad sketches of context and background, refraining—as far as I am able—from introducing later interpretations and formal ecclesiastical doctrine. It has been my intention to allow Jesus to speak for himself with as little interruption from me as can be managed. My commentary has therefore been a minimal one and confined to the introductory essays, apart from a few necessary footnotes to make clear what might otherwise be obscure.

I have used the Revised Standard Version text throughout this section. It is a widely-respected and comparatively recent version, authorized for liturgical use in both Roman Catholic and Anglican Churches and in widespread use among the Free Churches. It uses a good Greek text and adheres closely to the Greek word order. For the purposes of presenting the teachings of Jesus in their poetically constructed form, it is admirable.

In respect of the poetry, I am profoundly indebted to the work of a friend and colleague of twenty years standing, the late Dom Robert Petitpierre of Nashdom Abbey, and have made the fullest use of his two-volume work *Poems of Jesus* (Faith Press, 1965), for which I have been grateful ever since its appearance. For a detailed study of the poetic construction of many of the sayings of Jesus, the reader is referred to that work. However, a reading of familiar texts in such an unfamiliar presentation will very quickly reveal their poetic balance and structure, even through translation from Aramaic to Greek to English.

In dealing with biblical texts, it has become the fashion—at times nearly an obsession—to quote chapter and verse. This is a curiously modern custom—modern in terms of the biblical time-scale—as the chapter and verse numberings as we now know them date only from the early sixteenth century. Jesus decidedly did not quote references as he spoke, and so I have refrained from doing so in this anthology. In the first place I felt it unnecessary, and in the second place it seemed to me that a clutter of references and cross-references after every item would introduce just that kind of 'biblicism' that I have been most anxious to avoid.

I have therefore done something rather different; I have indicated after each item the generally accepted Source from which it is believed to have come; that is to say, 'Q', 'L', 'M', and so on. This has its own interest value, but it must be remembered that the last word has not been spoken by New Testament scholars in this matter (and will probably never be spoken, or scholarship will cease!) and that agreement on *this* or about *that* may not be absolute.

It must also be remembered that a great many of Jesus' teachings in the Gospels are recorded twice, and sometimes thrice, in different Gospels, with often a good measure of variation, both in presentation and in text. What follows in this part of the anthology is by far the greater part of those teachings of Jesus that are not either inextricably enmeshed in narrative, or in dialogue, but with very little duplication.

Thus, material marked 'Q' may come from either the Matthean or the Lukan version; material marked 'Mk' may come from the Markan, Matthean, or Lukan presentations of it. This in itself is of no consequence as far as the present work is concerned. Material marked 'M', 'L', and 'Jn' is from those sources peculiar to Matthew, Luke, and John respectively.

A final word of warning. The four gospels give us a remarkable 'stereoscopic' picture of Jesus, his ministry, and his personality. The remembered teachings are presented in the context of that picture by all four Evangelists, each one distinct and very different. Their joint concern was with *who he is* and *what God has done in him*. Thus the narrative is as important as the teachings.

Our present exercise, that of anthologizing the teachings, is rarely attempted, and perhaps the most venerable anthologizer (without narrative and context within it) was the unknown compiler of the apocryphal gospel of Thomas whose work we shall encounter in the second part of this anthology. His work is suspect in that it bears the marks of distortion in favour of a particular view, and any anthology must be coloured to some degree by the anthologizer.

The present compiler is exceedingly conscious of this danger and therefore solemnly renounces any such intention, consciously or unconsciously, to influence by presentation. Let Jesus speak for himself. In the words of St John the Baptist:

> He must increase,
> but I must decrease.

3

TWO RECURRING THEMES

THROUGHOUT the whole corpus of the recorded sayings of Jesus, two themes predominate. The first is that Truth, that Reality which he saw as his prime task to proclaim; the second is his own understanding of himself, of what we may best describe as his *persona*. The two are inseparable; the Reality, the fundamental Truth, and the Persona are inextricably bound up in each other. Let it be said at once that both are somewhat of an enigma. Both are provocative of endless debate among scholars. Jesus will never do another man's thinking for him; he invariably demands a personal, creative response both to himself and to what he has to say.

The first theme, the Reality he came to proclaim, has traditionally been rendered in English by the word *Kingdom*. Jesus proclaims the Kingdom of God or, as the First gospel has it, the Kingdom of Heaven. But in the late twentieth century the word *Kingdom* is not as helpful as once it might have been. It is an ambiguous term and a trifle archaic. We need to go back, if we can, to the words Jesus actually used and discover his meaning from there.

The New Testament, written in Greek, which was the *lingua franca* of the Eastern part of the Roman Empire, uses the word *Basileia*. This word corresponds to the English *Kingdom,* with all its ambiguity. There can be no doubt, however, that the word that Jesus used was the Aramaic *Malkutha* (Hebrew, *Malkuth*), which had a well-established and clear usage. It refers not to territorial jurisdication, but to a state of affairs, to sovereignty or kingly rule. A good English rendering might be *Reign* and, as sovereignty is not exercised in a void, the word *Realm* occasionally applies.*

The Malkuth of God—the Malkuth of Heaven as the first Gospel prefers—is what Jesus came, not merely to proclaim but *to inaugurate*. It was his role as inaugurator which makes it impossible to separate

---

*The Moffatt translation of the New Testament uses the words 'reign' and 'realm' to express what is meant by the Malkuth.

the Malkuth from his *persona*. The Hebrew language, Aramaic being its living form in the first century, is one which demands vivid, immediate, pictorial expression. Unlike Greek it does not deal in abstracts, nor can it articulate intricate philosophical concepts. Nevertheless, in the vividness, the poetry of Jesus we are invited to believe that *a whole new state of human affairs has arisen*. Central to it is the person of Jesus himself, the persona that he recognizes himself to be.

This persona, this second recurring theme, is translated in English as *The Son of Man*. The English is as literal a translation of the Greek *huios tou anthrōpou* as the latter is a literal translation of the Aramaic *Bar Nasha*—Son of Man. In the Synoptic Gospels particularly, Jesus is recorded as referring to himself in the third person as the Son of Man. Rarely does he use the first person and hardly ever is the expression, Son of Man, used of him by others. There is no serious reason for doubting that this is genuine reporting and that this title, this persona, was his own deliberately chosen description of himself. There were others that his followers, both regular and casual, sought to apply to him, but this was the one he chose for himself. The question now arises: what did he mean by it? How are we to interpret this persona, the Son of Man?

The Bible is full of 'son of' and 'sons of'. The young apostles James and John quickly acquired a nickname from Jesus; he called them 'sons of thunder' because of their fiery and impulsive natures. The Old Testament frequently makes reference to 'Sons of Belial', which we could render variously as 'sons of worthlessness', 'sons of destruction', 'sons of wickedness'. It is a vivid, poetic idiom, much more so than the contemporary description of the ill-behaved as 'rowdies' or 'vandals'. By the same token it is a more accurate description of the persons concerned. The centurion commanding the guard at the crucifixion of Jesus described him as having been a 'son of God'. By this he meant that Jesus had been a truly righteous and godly person. Elsewhere we read of 'sons of Adam' meaning the human race, and of 'sons of (or children of) Israel' meaning the Jewish people. The usage is poetic and at the same time perfectly clear without the slightest hint of precise definition.

Jesus' own use of the term 'Son of Man' is not quite like this, however. He is not describing himself as the 'the man in the street', which might be one contemporary translation of one of its meanings. It is a term much met with in the writings of the Prophets, in particular in Ezekiel, and used by the prophets of themselves as persons in receipt of divine inspiration and under divine obedience. 'Son of man, say this . . . Son of man, do that . . .'. This is how they often report God's words to them. A more fruitful source of understanding even than this comes from later books of the Old Testament and in particular the Book of Daniel, in which the writer records a mystical vision granted to him in which he saw 'the Ancient of days' (i.e. God) with, in His presence, a 'Son of Man'. The vision may be variously interpreted. In the context in which Daniel was written it is possible to argue that the 'Son of Man' was an archetypal figure representing the Jewish people, chosen by God and set apart among men. Be that as it may, there are also to be found various other, later understandings of the 'Son of Man' as a personal intervention by God into the affairs of mankind, not so much as a messenger but as an inaugurator of a state of affairs among men in which the Reign of God is specifically exercised.

Now it must be emphasized that all this is vague, enigmatic, and everlastingly debatable at an academic level. No precision of definition is to be found because beloved though such things are to our own day and age, precision of definition is foreign to the whole *ambience* of Jesus. He cannot be pinned down within such a narrow, two-dimensional compass. Life is bigger than that! And precision of definition could issue only in half-truths and falsehoods. In Jesus we are dealing with a poet who knows, as none others could know, that only poetry can give—indeed suggest—expression to the heights, the depths, the 'wholly other' that the Son of Man challenges us, with the utmost urgency, to respond to in his relentless proclamation of the Malkuth of God.

❧

The kingdom of heaven shall be compared to ten maidens who took their lamps and went to meet the bridegroom. Five of them were foolish, and five were wise. For when the foolish took their lamps, they took no oil with them; but the wise took flasks of oil with their lamps. As the bridegroom was delayed, they all slumbered and slept. But at midnight there was a cry, 'Behold, the bridegroom! Come out to meet him.' Then all those maidens rose and trimmed their lamps. And the foolish said to the wise, 'Give us some of your oil, for our lamps are going out.' But the wise replied, 'Perhaps there will not be enough for us and for you; go rather to the dealers and buy for yourselves.' And while they went to buy, the bridegroom came, and those who were ready went in with him to the marriage feast; and the door was shut. Afterward the other maidens came also, saying, 'Lord, Lord, open to us.' But he replied, 'Truly, I say to you, I do not know you.' Watch therefore, for you know neither the day nor the hour.

(M)

The kingdom of heaven is like
treasure hidden in a field,
which a man found and covered up;
then in his joy he goes
and sells all that he has
and buys that field.

Again, the kingdom of heaven is like
a merchant in search of fine pearls,
who, on finding one pearl of great value,
went,
and sold all that he had
and bought it.

(M)

What is the kingdom of God like? And to what shall I compare it? It is like a grain of mustard seed which a man took and sowed in his garden; and it grew and became a tree, and the birds of the air made nests in its branches.

(Q)

No one has ascended
into heaven
but he who has descended
from heaven,
the Son of man.

(Jn)

The kingdom of heaven may be compared to a man who sowed good seed in his field; but while men were sleeping, his enemy came and sowed weeds among the wheat, and went away. So when the plants came up and bore grain, then the weeds appeared also. And the servants of the householder came and said to him, 'Sir, did you not sow good seed in your field? How then has it weeds?' He said to them, 'An enemy has done this.' The servants said to him, 'Then do you want us to go and gather them?' But he said, 'No; lest in gathering the weeds you root up the wheat along with them. Let both grow together until the harvest; and at harvest time I will tell the reapers, Gather the weeds first and bind them in bundles to be burned, but gather the wheat into my barn.'

(M)

Truly, truly, I say to you,

a servant is not greater
than his master;
nor is he who is sent greater
than he who sent him.

(Jn)

What if you were to see the Son of man ascending where he was before? It is the spirit that gives life, the flesh is of no avail; the words that I have spoken to you are spirit and life. But there are some of you that do not believe.

(Jn)

I have come as light
into the world,
that whoever believes in me
may not remain in darkness.

(Jn)

The kingdom of God is not coming with signs to be observed; nor will they say, 'Lo, here it is!' or 'There!' for behold, the kingdom of God is in the midst of you.

(L)

When you have lifted up the Son of man, then you will know that I am he, and that I do nothing on my own authority, but speak thus as the Father taught me. And he who sent me is with me; he has not left me alone, for I always do what is pleasing to him.

(Jn)

You know that those who are supposed
to rule over the Gentiles
lord it over them,
and their great men
exercise authority over them.
But it shall not be so
among you;

but whoever would be great among you
must be your servant,
and whoever would be first among you
must be slave of all.

For the Son of man also came
not to be served
but to serve,
and to give his life
as a ransom for many.

(Mk)

The kingdom of heaven is like a net which was thrown into the sea
and gathered fish of every kind; when it was full, men drew it ashore
and sat down and sorted the good into vessels but threw away the bad.

(M)

O Jerusalem, Jerusalem,
killing
the prophets
and stoning
those who are sent to you!

How often would I have gathered
your children together
as a hen gathers
her brood under her wings,

and you would not!

(Q)

The days are coming when you will desire to see one of the days of
the Son of man, and you will not see it. And they will say to you

'Lo, there!' or 'Lo, here!' Do not go, do not follow them. For as the lightning flashes and lights up the sky from one side to the other, so will the Son of man be in his days. But first he must suffer many things and be rejected by this generation.

(Q)

The kingdom of heaven is like a householder who went out early in the morning to hire labourers for his vineyard. After agreeing with the labourers for a denarius a day, he sent them into his vineyard. And going out about the third hour he saw others standing idle in the market place; and to them he said, 'You go into the vineyard too, and whatever is right I will give you.' So they went. Going out again about the sixth hour and the ninth hour he did the same. And about the eleventh hour he went out and found others standing; and he said to them, 'Why do you stand here idle all day?' They said to him, 'Because no one has hired us.' He said to them, 'You go into the vineyard too.' And when evening came, the owner of the vineyard said to his steward, 'Call the labourers and pay them their wages, beginning with the last, up to the first.' And when those hired about the eleventh hour came, each of them received a denarius. Now when the first came, they thought they would receive more; but each of them also received a denarius. And on receiving it they grumbled at the householder, saying, 'These last worked only one hour, and you have made them equal to us who have borne the burden of the day and the scorching heat.' But he replied to one of them, 'Friend, I am doing you no wrong; did you not agree with me for a denarius? Take what belongs to you, and go; I choose to give to this last as I give to you. Am I not allowed to do what I choose with what belongs to me? Or do you begrudge my generosity?' So the last will be first, and the first last.

(M)

Those who are well
have no need of a physician,
but those who are sick;

I came
not to call the righteous,
but sinners.

(Mk)

To what shall I compare the kingdom of God? It is like leaven which
a woman took and hid in three measures of meal, till it was all leavened.

(Q)

You know me,
and you know where I come from.

But I have not come of my own accord;
he who sent me is true,
and him you do not know.

I know him,
for I come from him,
and he sent me.

(Jn)

Truly, truly, I say to you,

before Abraham was,
I am.

(Jn)

Truly, truly, I say to you,

you will see heaven opened,
and the angels of God
ascending
and descending
upon the Son of man.

(Jn)

If I bear witness to myself,
my testimony is not true;
there is another who bears witness to me,
and I know that the testimony which he bears to me is true.

You sent to John,*
and he has borne witness to the truth.
Not that the testimony which I receive is from man;
but I say this that you may be saved.
He was a burning and shining lamp,
and you were willing to rejoice for a while in his light.

*John the Baptist.

But the testimony which I have
is greater than that of John;

for the works which the Father has granted me to
    accomplish,
these very works which I am doing,
bear me witness
that the Father has sent me.
And the Father who sent me
has himself borne witness to me.

His voice
you have never heard,
his form
you have never seen;
and his word
you do not have abiding in you,

for him whom he has sent
you do not believe.

(Jn)

Truly, truly, I say to you, unless one is born anew, he cannot see the kingdom of God.

(Jn)

If I tell you,
you will not believe;
and if I ask you,
you will not answer.

But from now on
the Son of man shall be seated
at the right hand of the power of God.

(L)

4

CONFLICT

ANYONE who has lived and worked in a multi-lingual, multi-racial, and multi-cultural society, such as may be found in both the Near East and the Far East, will be familiar with the way in which useful words and phrases pass between one language and another, especially where there are meanings and associations articulated vividly in one language but not in another.

'Galilee of the Nations' was such a society, with Aramaic-speaking and Greek-speaking villages close to each other, with a main highway passing through, and with all the people jumbled up together in the market places. However tightly a group hangs on to its language and identity, there is a bi-lingual or multi-lingual *ambiance* which we can never now recover in the case of first-century Palestine. Daily papers, women's magazines, popular journalism, did not exist. The texts available to scholars cannot convey the popular scene of the times.

We cannot ever know, therefore, to what extent the writer of the Fourth Gospel was translating or interpreting when he reports Jesus as using the Greek word *kosmos*. The word means both 'order' and 'the world' (or universe). As such it has passed into English. Cosmos means the ordered universe; it is contrasted with another Greek word, Chaos, which means total disorder.

Was the gospel writer translating from Aramaic with a rare sublety, or had Jesus taken that foreign (but well-known) word into his vocabulary for the sake of its useful meaning and associations? We don't know, but the way in which it is used displays a profound and subtle irony. For Jesus, Cosmos, the ordered world, is but skin deep. Scratch the surface and what do you find? The answer is: Chaos!

Cosmos, for Jesus, is that ordered world of armed truces which men call peace, the whole fabric of false human values, the aura of half-truths, falsehoods, respectable corruptions, and all-pervading dishonesty which seems perpetually to overshadow the human condition—which indeed *is* the human condition. Cosmos is but Chaos with a coat of whitewash.

The Fourth Gospel, recording the more intimate conversations between Jesus and his disciples which the Synoptics do not give us, shows us a vivid picture of Jesus and 'the world' at total odds one with the other. It is a mortal combat that is being waged.

The Synoptics reveal Jesus as being totally at odds with both the religious establishment and the attitudes of the most conventional and respectable religious people. Almost at once we understand the most apparently devout people in the community to be conspiring to get rid of Jesus. In the Fourth Gospel, the conflicts are fiercest in the very Temple precincts. In the end, when Jesus was judicially murdered, he was got rid of because he was a threat to religion. Political considerations were involved, but the religious were paramount.

For Jesus there can be no distinction whatsoever between 'the sacred' and 'the secular'. Nothing is secular; all is sacred, for all is God's. There can be no distinction between 'religion' and 'life' for all Life is One and it all comes from God. All the thinking, and the attitudes, which create artificial categories, setting life at odds with itself, belong to 'the world'. Jesus was quite clear that his mission was to do battle with, and to overthrow, 'the prince of this world'.

The Old Testament, in its Creation mythology, brilliantly articulated a profound understanding that man is a creature suffering from what might be described as a congenital deformity of the will. The principle of disorder is in him, against which he is powerless, even though he recognizes his case. This principle of disorder, something other than man himself, proceeding from beyond him in some way or other, the Old Testament personalizes under the figure of the primeval serpent, Satan, and, in Jesus' own words, 'the father of lies', 'the prince of this world'. The conflict in which Jesus is engaged—which his very presence engenders—is therefore to be understood as present on many levels and in more dimensions than we can properly comprehend.

'The world', the value-system, *kosmos*, is but the manifestation in human affairs of that principle of disorder, the very nature of which is Chaos and the end-product of which is Death.

Jesus saw himself as having entered the realm of Death in order to overthrow Death and bring new and authentic Life. He had no illusions that this was the ultimate of Life and Death struggles and that he himself would be the battleground. He had no illusions as to the cost of the struggle for himself.

Do not think that I have come
to bring peace
on earth;

I have not come
to bring peace,
but a sword;

For I have come
to set a man
against his father,
and a daughter
against her mother,
and a daughter-in-law
against her mother-in-law;

and a man's foes will be
those of his own household.

(Q)

My time
has not yet come,
but your time
is always here.

The world cannot hate you,
but it hates me
because I testify of it
that its works are evil.

Go to the feast yourselves;
I am not going up to this feast,

for my time
has not yet fully come.

(Jn)

Now is the judgement of this world;
now shall the ruler of this world* be cast out;
and I,
when I am lifted up from the earth
will draw all men to myself.

(Jn)

*The Devil.

I came to cast fire upon the earth;
and would that it were already kindled!
I have a baptism to be baptized with;
and how I am constrained until it is accomplished!

(Q)

Why do you not understand
what I say?
It is because you cannot bear to hear
my word.

You
are of your father the devil,
and your will is to do
your father's desires.

He was a murderer from the beginning,
and has nothing to do with the truth,
because there is no truth in him.
When he lies,
he speaks according to his own nature,
for he is a liar,
and the father of lies.

But because I tell the truth
you do not believe me.
Which of you
convicts me of sin?
If I tell the truth,
why do you not believe me?

He who is of God
hears the words of God;
the reason you do not hear them
is that you are not of God.

(Jn)

I honour my Father, and you dishonour me. Yet I do not seek my
own glory; there is One who seeks it and he will be the judge.

(Jn)

I do not receive glory from men.
But I know that you have not the love of God within you.

I have come
in my Father's name,
and you do not receive me;

if another comes
in his own name,
him you will receive.

How can you believe,
who receive glory
from one another
and do not seek the glory
that comes from the only God?

(Jn)

You hypocrites!

Does not each of you on the sabbath
untie his ox or his ass from the manger,
and lead it away to water it?

And ought not this woman,*
a daughter of Abraham
whom Satan bound for eighteen years,
be loosed from this bond
on the sabbath day?

(L)

If you were Abraham's children,
you would do what Abraham did,
but now you seek to kill me,
a man who has told you the truth
which I heard from God;
this is not what Abraham did.
You do what your father did.

(Jn)

*A woman, member of a synagogue congregation and suffering from
curvature of the spine, who was healed by Jesus amid uproar at his 'sabbath-
breaking'.

To what then shall I compare the men of this generation,
and what are they like?

They are like children sitting in the market place
calling to one another,
'We piped to you,
'and you did not dance;
'we wailed,
'and you did not weep.'

For John the Baptist has come
eating no bread and drinking no wine;
and you say,
'He has a demon.'

The Son of man has come
eating and drinking;
and you say,
'Behold a glutton and a drunkard,
'a friend of tax collectors and sinners!'

Yet wisdom is justified
by all her children.

(Q)

You know neither me
nor my Father;
if you knew me,
you would know my Father also.

(Jn)

Do not give dogs what is holy;
and do not throw your pearls before swine.
lest they trample them underfoot
and turn to attack you.

(M)

For this reason the Father loves me,
because I lay down my life,
that I may take it again.
No one takes it from me,
but I lay it down of my own accord.

I have power to lay it down,
and I have power to take it again;
this charge I have received from my Father.

(Jn)

I go away,
and you will seek me
and die in your sin;

where I am going,
you cannot come.

(Jn)

Now is the Son of man glorified,
and in him God is glorified;

if God is glorified in him,
God will also glorify him in himself,
and glorify him at once.

(Jn)

The poems that conclude this section, 'The Beelzebul Poems', as they may be styled, concern the conflict with what might be called archetypal evil which was the fundamental conflict of the life and ministry of Jesus. The Adversary is Satan, sometimes called Beelzebul *(a Philistine god, worshipped at Ekron, whose name had been applied to 'prince of the devils'), and also known to Jesus as the prince, or ruler of 'this world'.*

How can Satan cast out Satan?

If a kingdom
is divided against itself,
that kingdom cannot stand.

And if a house
is divided against itself,
that house will not be able to stand.

And if Satan
has risen against himself
and is divided,
he cannot stand,
but is coming to an end.

(Mk)

Every kingdom
divided against itself
is laid waste,

and no city or house
divided against itself
will stand;

and if Satan casts out Satan,
he is divided against himself;
how then will his kingdom stand?

(Probably M)

You say that I cast out demons
by Beelzebul.
And if I cast out demons
by Beelzebul,
by whom
do your sons cast them out?

Therefore they
shall be your judges.

But if it is by the finger of God
that I cast out demons,
then the kingdom of God
has come upon you.

(Q)

But no man can enter a strong man's house
and plunder his goods,
unless he first binds the strong man;
then indeed he may plunder his house.

(Mk)

When a strong man, fully armed,
guards his own palace,
his goods are in peace;

but when one stronger than he
assails him
and overcomes him,

he takes away his armour
in which he trusted,
and divides his spoil.

(Q)

He who is not with me
is against me,
and he who does not gather with me
scatters.

(Q)

Truly, I say to you

all sins will be forgiven the sons of men,
and whatever blasphemies they utter;
but whoever blasphemes against the Holy Spirit
never has forgiveness

but is guilty of an eternal sin.

(Mk)

Therefore I tell you,
every sin and blasphemy
will be forgiven men,
but the blasphemy against the Spirit
will not be forgiven.

And whoever says a word against the Son of man
will be forgiven;
but whoever speaks against the Holy Spirit
will not be forgiven,

either in this age
or in the age to come.

(Probably M)

When the unclean spirit has gone out of a man,
he passes through waterless places
seeking rest;
and finding none
he says, 'I will return to my house
'from which I came.'

And when he comes
he finds it swept
and put in order.

Then he goes
and brings seven other spirits
more evil than himself,

and they enter
and dwell there;

and the last state of that man
becomes worse than the first.

(Q)

5

THE WAY

THERE is something about the Old Testament that is quite unique. It presents an altogether original understanding of the relationship between God and man.

As that great library that forms the Old Testament was being compiled, edited, and added to over at least a thousand years of written records, an understanding emerged which was quite different from any other among the emerging great religions of mankind.

A *process* was going on. History has meaning. There is growth, development, emergence. There is a sense of specific vocation for a purpose. The relationship between God and man is first of all *personal,* but it is, like all personal relationships, progressive, on-going, developing all the time, moving towards a fulfilment. This is the essential message of the Old Testament which was, needless to say, the Bible as far as Jesus was concerned.

This dynamic theology stood in vivid contrast to its contemporaries in other religions; in particular we may think of the great religions of the Far East. The three or four generations in the sixth and seventh centuries BC which produced Gautama Buddha, Confucius, Lao-Tse, and the writer of the second part of the prophecy of Isaiah produced, in the East, a sense of the order and wonder of the universe and the perversity of man (Lao-Tse), a sense of the disorder of human relationships and a brave attempt to define them (Confucius), and an overpowering sense of the enslaving power of human desires and of the world misery they cause (Buddha). In the West, within the already perceived personal relationship between God and man, and the moral order that this demands, Isaiah understood that the 'God of Israel' was no tribal archetype but the Creator of Heaven and Earth. He perceived the universal brotherhood of man within the Fatherhood of God, and that this relationship was dynamic and moving towards a fulfilment of some kind.

It need not surprise us, therefore, that the understanding of the Old Testament concerning the relationship between God and man should find expression in dynamic rather than static concepts. And so, over and over again, we find use made of such words as 'The Way'.

In Old Testament usage, 'The Way' is used to describe a road, or a journey. It is also used to describe human conduct or character, either good or bad. And it is used to describe the creative power of God, the moral rule of God, the commandments of God.

The Old Testament provided Jesus with his context, his vocabulary, his thought-forms. 'The Way' therefore passes into the Gospels and the rest of the New Testament, but with some very important developments.

The Fourth Gospel reports a startling modification. The Apostle Thomas, quite bewildered and exasperated at being unable to grasp the sense of Jesus' words on one occasion, burst out: 'Lord; we don't know where you are going; how can we know the way?' The answer he got is of fundamental importance. Jesus replied; 'I am the way!'

To his disciples, but not to the general public, Jesus is reported as claiming to be the uniting principle of Heaven and Earth, of God and man. Needless to say, Jesus himself defined no doctrines. Mystery is incapable of definition and Jesus never did another man's thinking for him. Jesus was a poet who knew as nobody else knew how poetry alone can hint at an expression of the utterly inexpressible. To press definition further is to end up with a half-truth.

The followers of Jesus, both the immediate followers and the later ones, were quick to grasp the implication. But it is important to remember that it was *their experience of Jesus* rather than his words as such which taught them. Jesus was recognized as being himself 'the Good News'. He himself is 'the Way' and was seen as having opened 'the way', the 'way of the Lord' in its fulfilment. To use a technical theological term, he was recognized as 'the Saviour'.

What is a 'Saviour?' Quite simply, 'the helper'. The one who makes it possible for the Way to be found and followed; who is in himself the 'way' itself; road, journey, character, commandment, reign.

Truly, truly, I say to you,

I am the door of the sheep.
All who came before me
are thieves and robbers;
but the sheep did not heed them.

I am the door;
if any one enters by me,
he will be saved,
and will go in and out
and find pasture.

The thief comes
only to steal
and kill and destroy;

I came
that they may have life,
and have it abundantly.

(Jn)

Come to me,
all who labour
and are heavy laden,
and I will give you rest.

Take my yoke upon you,
and learn from me;
for I am gentle
and lowly in heart,
and you will find rest for your souls.

For my yoke is easy,
and my burden is light.

(M)

I am the good shepherd.
The good shepherd lays down his life for the sheep.

He who is a hireling and not a shepherd,
whose own the sheep are not,
sees the wolf coming
and leaves the sheep
and flees;
and the wolf snatches them,
and scatters them.

He flees
because he is a hireling
and cares nothing for the sheep.

I am the good shepherd;
I know my own,
and my own know me
and I know the Father;
and I lay down my life for the sheep.

(Jn)

Therefore do not be anxious
about tomorrow,
for tomorrow
will be anxious for itself.

(M)

What man of you, having a hundred sheep,
if he has lost one of them,
does not leave the ninety-nine in the wilderness,
and go after the one which is lost,
until he finds it?

And when he has found it,
he lays it on his shoulders, rejoicing.
And when he comes home,
he calls together his friends and his neighbours,
saying to them,
'Rejoice with me,
'for I have found my sheep which was lost.'

Just so, I tell you,
there will be more joy in heaven
over one sinner who repents
than over ninety-nine righteous persons
who need no repentance.

Or what woman, having ten silver coins,
if she loses one coin,
does not light a lamp
and sweep the house
and seek diligently
until she finds it?

And when she has found it,
she calls together her friends and neighbours,
saying,
'Rejoice with me,
'for I have found the coin which I had lost.'

Just so, I tell you,
there is joy before the angels of God
over one sinner who repents.

(L)

My teaching
is not mine,
but his who sent me;

if any man's will
is to do his will,

he shall know whether the teaching
is from God
or whether I am speaking on my own authority.

He who speaks on his own authority
seeks his own glory;
but he who seeks the glory
of him who sent him

is true
and in him there is no falsehood.

(Jn)

Truly, truly, I say to you,

he who does not enter the sheepfold by the door
but climbs in by another way,
that man is a thief and a robber.

But he who enters by the door
is the shepherd of the sheep.

To him the gatekeeper opens;
the sheep hear his voice,
and he calls his own sheep by name
and leads them out.
When he has brought out all his own,
he goes before them,

and the sheep follow him,
for they know his voice.

A stranger they will not follow,
but they will flee from him,
for they do not know the voice of strangers.

(Jn)

What man of you, if he has one sheep and it falls into a pit on the sabbath, will not lay hold of it and lift it out? Of how much more value is a man than a sheep! So it is lawful to do good on the sabbath.

(M)

The sabbath was made
for man,
not man
for the sabbath;

so the Son of man
is lord even of the sabbath.

(Mk)

Do not be anxious about your life,
what you shall eat,
nor about your body,
what you shall put on.
For life
is more than food,
and the body
more than clothing.

Consider the ravens:
they neither sow nor reap,
they have neither storehouse nor barn,
and yet Gods feeds them.

Of how much more value are you than the birds!

And which of you by being anxious
can add a cubit to his span of life?
If then you are not able to do as small a thing as that,
why are you anxious about the rest?

Consider the lilies, how they grow;
they neither toil nor spin;
yet I tell you,
even Solomon in all his glory
was not arrayed like one of these.

But if God so clothes the grass
which is alive in the field today,
and tomorrow is thrown into the oven,
how much more will he clothe you, O men of little faith!

And do not seek what you are to eat
and what you are to drink,
nor be of anxious mind.

For all the nations of the world
seek these things;
and your Father knows
that you need them.

Instead, seek his kingdom,
and these things shall be yours as well.

(Q)

You call me
Teacher and Lord;
and you are right,
for so I am.

If I then, your Lord and Teacher,
have washed
your feet,

you also
ought to wash
one another's feet.

For I have given you an example,
that you should do
as I have done to you.

(Jn)

I entered your house,

You gave me no water for my feet,
but she has wet my feet with her tears*
and wiped them with her hair.

You gave me no kiss,
but from the time I came in she
has not ceased to kiss my feet.

You did not anoint my head with oil,
but she has anointed my feet with ointment.

Therefore I tell you,

her sins, which are many, are forgiven,
for she loved much;
but he who is forgiven little,
loves little.

(L)

Moses gave you circumcision
(not that it is from Moses,
but from the fathers),
and you circumcise a man
upon the sabbath.

If on the sabbath
a man receives circumcision,
so that the law of Moses may not be broken,

are you angry with me
because on the sabbath
I made a man's whole body well?

Do not judge by appearances,
but judge with right judgement.

(Jn)

*A penitent harlot who gatecrashed a dinner party, given for Jesus by
a leading Pharisee.

Take heed, and beware of all covetousness; for a man's life does not consist in the abundance of his possessions.

(L)

Either make the tree good,
and its fruit good;
or make the tree bad,
and its fruit bad;
for the tree is known
by its fruit.

You brood of vipers!
how can you speak good
when you are evil?
For out of the abundance of the heart
the mouth speaks.

The good man
out of his good treasure
brings forth good,
and the evil man
out of his evil treasure
brings forth evil.

I tell you,
on the day of judgement
men will render account
for every careless word they utter;

for by your words you will be justified,
and by your words you will be condemned.

(M)

Are there not twelve hours in the day?

If any one walks in the day,
he does not stumble,
because he sees the light of this world.

But if any one walks in the night,
he stumbles,
because the light is not in him.

(Jn)

Beware of practising your piety before men
in order to be seen by them;
for then you will have no reward
from your Father who is in heaven.

Thus, when you give alms,
sound no trumpet before you
as the hypocrites do
in the synagogues and in the streets,
that they may be praised by men.
Truly, I say to you, they have their reward.

But when you give alms,
do not let your left hand know
what your right hand is doing,
so that your alms may be in secret;
and your Father who sees in secret
will reward you.

And when you pray,
you must not be like the hypocrites;
for they love to stand and pray
in the synagogue and at the street corners,
that they may be seen by men.
Truly, I say to you, they have their reward.

But when you pray,
go into your room
and shut the door
and pray to your Father who is in secret;

and your Father who sees in secret
will reward you.

And when you fast,
do not look dismal,
like the hypocrites,
for they disfigure their faces
that their fasting may be seen by men.
Truly, I say to you, they have their reward.

But when you fast,
anoint your head and wash your face,
that your fasting may not be seen by men
but by your Father who sees in secret;

and your Father who sees in secret
will reward you.

(M)

Are not five sparrows sold for two pennies?
And not one of them is forgotten before God.
Why, even the hairs of your head are all numbered.
Fear not; you are of more value than many sparrows.

(Q)

When you are invited by any one to a marriage feast,
do not sit down in a place of honour,
lest a more eminent man than you
be invited by him;
and he who invited you both will come
and say to you, 'Give place to this man',
and then you will begin with shame
to take the lowest place.

But when you are invited,
go and sit in the lowest place,
so that when your host comes
he may say to you, 'Friend, go up higher';
then you will be honoured
in the presence of all who sit at table with you.

For everyone who exalts himself
will be humbled,
and he who humbles himself
will be exalted.

(L)

Give
to him who begs from you,
and do not refuse
to him who would borrow from you.

(M—but possibly Q)

As you go with your accuser before the magistrate, make an effort to settle with him on the way, lest he drag you to the judge, and the judge hand you over to the officer, and the officer put you in prison. I tell you, you will never get out till you have paid the very last copper.

(Q)

Do not swear at all,

either by heaven,
for it is the throne of God,
or by the earth,
for it is his footstool,
or by Jerusalem,
for it is the city of the great King.

And do not swear by your head,
for you cannot make one hair white or black.

Let what you say
be simply 'Yes' or 'No';
anything more than this
comes from evil.

(Mk)

Love your enemies
and pray for those who persecute you,
so that you may be sons
of your Father who is in heaven;

for he makes his sun rise
on the evil and on the good,
and sends rain
on the just and on the unjust.

(M)

Whatever you wish that men should do to you, do so to them; for this is the law and the prophets.

(M)

When you give a dinner or a banquet,
do not invite your friends or your brothers
or your kinsmen or rich neighbours,

lest they also invite you in return,
and you be repaid.

But when you give a feast,
invite the poor, the maimed,
the lame, the blind,

and you will be blessed,
because they cannot repay you.

You will be repaid
at the resurrection of the just.

(L)

It is more blessed
to give
than to receive.

(Quoted by St Paul in the Acts of the Apostles)

If your brother sins,
rebuke him,
and if he repents,
forgive him;

and if he sins against you
seven times in the day,
and turns to you
seven times,
and says, 'I repent',
you must forgive him.

(Q)

These things I have spoken to you,
that my joy
may be in you,
and that your joy
may be full.

(Jn)

6

RESPONSIBILITY

'WHY was atheism created?' asked a traditional Jewish Rabbi. He answered his own question: 'So that we should not rely only on God, when we work in the world, but carry on as if He did not exist, and the responsibility was on our shoulders alone.'[1]

The whole biblical understanding of mankind centres upon the idea of responsibility. First and foremost, man is a *responsible* creature. This is what is meant by the biblical doctrine of man as being created in the 'image and likeness of God'.

Responsibility is not exercised in a vacuum, however. It is necessary for there to be something to be responsible *for*, and someone to be responsible *to*. And man is given responsibility for the world in which he dwells. He is told; 'fill the earth and subdue it, and have dominion.' He is responsible for his fellow-men and women. 'Am I my brother's keeper?' asked Cain, the first murderer. He discovered that indeed he was, and was held responsible. Man is responsible for his own integrity, as Adam and Eve discovered as soon as they had lost theirs. The Creation mythology of the Bible sets the stage and establishes the context of mankind very clearly, with both subtlety and humour. But the responsibility of mankind is total.

Man is responsible to God whose manager he is. Like his Creator he is himself creative. According to his own place in the scheme of things he is co-creator with God in the course of the fulfilment of his humanity. He is responsible to his fellow men and women, and he is responsible to himself, all within his overall responsibility to God who gave him his being.

Responsibility therefore is the supreme characteristic of manhood and womanhood. The irresponsible are *failing in their humanity*. Integrity is bound up with responsibility and it was, quite simply, irresponsibility that was the great sin of Adam and Eve.

Obedience and disobedience are categories that belong to a

[1] Lionel Blue, *To Heaven with Scribes and Pharisees* (DLT, 1975), p. 23.

relationship between unequal persons. There can be no equality between creature and Creator, and yet Jesus calls mankind to that equality as something freely given. It is to be a partnership between equals in which Jesus is, ideally, *primus inter pares*: first among equals. The calling is to a higher responsibility, transcending the categories of obedience and disobedience. The theme of responsibility constantly recurs. The obedient servant is praised over and over again, but the calling goes beyond such a relationship as master and servant. It is to the ultimate relationship of equals, that of friend and friend.

It is easier, and a great deal less alarming, to remain a servant or even a child, *and thus to evade the responsibility to which mankind is called.* A great deal of conventional piety seems to be directed towards this kind of evasion, and to perpetuate a relationship that Jesus calls mankind to grow out of. There is a religious paternalism which seeks to protect people from themselves lest they fall into error, and to keep believers in a perpetual state of pious childhood. This runs directly contrary to the call of Jesus to men and women to be bold enough to become true, authentic men and women, the New Humanity of which he is Archetype; 'the New Adam', as the early Church proclaimed him.

Humility is, quite simply, facing up to reality; the abandonment of all fantasy and self-deception. True humility and responsibility go hand in hand; they are what authentic humanity is about.

In their quest for authentic humanity, Christians have recognized in Jesus the Saviour, in other words the Helper, the Enabler. The Greek word for this is *kristos*, Christ.

That is why he is called Jesus Christ.

✧❦✧

Let your loins be girded and your lamps burning, and be like men who are waiting for their master to come home from the marriage feast, so that they may open to him at once when he comes and knocks. Blessed are those servants whom the master finds awake when he comes; truly, I say to you, he will gird himself and have them sit at table, and he will come and serve them. If he comes in the second watch, or in the third, and finds them so, blessed are those servants! But know this, that if the householder had known at what hour the thief was coming, he would have been awake and would not have left his house to be broken into. You also must be ready; for the Son of man is coming at an hour you do not expect.

(Q)

Beware of false prophets,
who come to you in sheep's clothing
but inwardly are ravening wolves.

You will know them by their fruits.
Are grapes gathered from thorns,
or figs from thistles?

So, every sound tree
bears good fruit,
but the bad tree
bears evil fruit.
A sound tree cannot bear evil fruit,
nor can a bad tree
bear good fruit.

Every tree that does not bear good fruit
is cut down and thrown into the fire.
Thus you will know them by their fruits.

(M)

This is my commandment,
that you
love one another
as I
have loved you.

Greater love has no man than this,
that a man lay down his life
for his friends.
You are my friends
if you do
what I command you.

No longer do I call you servants,
for the servant does not know
what his master is doing;

but I have called you friends,
for all that I have heard from my Father
I have made known to you.

You did not choose me,
but I chose you,
and appointed you
that you should go
and bear fruit,
and that your fruit
should abide;

so that whatever you ask the Father
in my name,
he may give it to you.

This I command you,
to love one another.

(Jn)

If you forgive men their trespasses, your heavenly Father also will forgive you; but if you do not forgive men their trespasses, neither will your Father forgive your trespasses.

(M)

Why do you see the speck
that is in your brother's eye,
but do not notice the log
that is in your own eye?

Or how can you say to your brother,
'Let me take the speck
'out of your eye,'
when there is the log
in your own eye?

You hypocrite,
first take the log
out of your own eye,
and then you will see clearly
to take the speck
out of your brother's eye.

(M)

There was a rich man, who was clothed in purple and fine linen and who feasted sumptuously every day. And at his gate lay a poor man named Lazarus, full of sores, who desired to be fed with what fell from the rich man's table; moreover the dogs came and licked his sores. The poor man died and was carried by the angels to Abraham's bosom. The rich man also died and was buried; and in Hades, being in torment, he lifted up his eyes, and saw Abraham far off and Lazarus in his bosom. And he called out, 'Father Abraham, have mercy upon me, and send Lazarus to dip the end of his finger in water and cool my tongue; for I am in anguish in this flame.' But Abraham said, 'Son, remember that you in your lifetime received your good things, and Lazarus in like manner evil things; but now he is comforted here, and you are in anguish. And besides all this, between us and you a great chasm has been fixed, in order that those who would pass from here to you may not be able, and none may cross from there to us.' And he said to him, 'Then I beg you, father, to send him to my father's house, for I have five brothers, so that he may warn them, lest they also come into this place of torment.' But Abraham said, 'They have Moses and the prophets; let them hear them.' And he said, 'No, father Abraham; but if some one goes to them from the dead, they will repent.' He said to him, 'If they do not hear Moses and the prophets, neither will they be convinced if some one should rise from the dead.'

(L)

Think not that I have come to abolish
the law and the prophets;
I have come not to abolish them
but to fulfil them.

For truly, I say to you,
till heaven and earth pass away,
not an iota, not a dot,
will pass from the law
until all is accomplished.

Whoever then relaxes one of the least of these
    commandments
and teaches men so,
shall be called least
in the kingdom of heaven;

but he who does them
and teaches them
shall be called great
in the kingdom of heaven.

For I tell you,
unless your righteousness
exceeds that of the scribes and Pharisees,
you will never enter
the kingdom of heaven.

(M)

Two men went up into the temple to pray, one a Pharisee and the other a tax collecter.* The Pharisee stood and prayed thus with himself, 'God, I thank thee that I am not like other men, extortioners, unjust, adulterers, or even like this tax collector. I fast twice a week, I give tithes of all that I get.' But the tax collector, standing far off, would not even lift up his eyes to heaven, but beat his breast, saying, 'God, be merciful to me a sinner.' I tell you, this man went down to his house justified rather than the other; for every one who exalts himself will be humbled, but he who humbles himself will be exalted.

(L)

If you love those who love you,
what credit is that to you?
For even sinners love those who love them.

And if you do good to those who do good to you,
what credit is that to you?
For even sinners do the same.

And if you lend to those from whom you hope to receive,
what credit is that to you?
Even sinners lend to sinners, to receive as much again.

*The two extremes, from the religious point of view. The Pharisees were the most pious, most observant of all Jews, whose failing was a tendency to make 'religion' into a god and rely on a kind of legal righteousness; thus if one faithfully observed every religious law according to the strictest interpretation, one was bound to be righteous! Spiritual pride comes easily to such a view. The tax collector, on the other hand, was a social and religious outcast, who had tendered for the job of collecting taxes for the occupying power on a commission basis. Tax collectors were thus universally despised and hated by their fellow-Jews and their profession was held to be almost synonymous with sin!

But love your enemies,
and do good,
and lend, expecting nothing in return;

and your reward will be great,
and you will be sons of the Most High;
for he is kind to the ungrateful and the selfish.

(Q)

Every one to whom much is given,
of him will much be required;
and of him to whom men commit much
they will demand the more.

(Q)

Will any one of you, who has a servant ploughing or keeping sheep,
say to him when he has come in from the field, 'Come at once and
sit down at table?' Will he not rather say to him, 'Prepare supper
for me, and gird yourself and serve me, till I eat and drink?' Does
he thank the servant because he did what was commanded? So you
also, when you have done all that is commanded you, say, 'We are
unworthy servants; we have only done what was our duty.'

(L)

No one can serve two masters;

for either he will hate the one,
and love the other,

or he will be devoted to the one,
and despise the other.

You cannot serve God and mammon.*

(M — possibly Q)

He who is faithful in a very little
is faithful also in much;
and he who is dishonest in a very little
is dishonest also in much.

*Mammon: a Semitic word of obscure origin which can be translated
as 'money' but is probably better rendered as 'the profit motive'.

If then you have not been faithful
in the unrighteous mammon,
who will entrust to you
the true riches?

And if you have not been faithful
in that which is another's,
who will give you
that which is your own?

(L)

A nobleman went into a far country to receive kingly power and then return. Calling ten of his servants, he gave them ten pounds, and said to them, 'Trade with these till I come.' But his citizens hated him and sent an embassy after him, saying, 'We do not want this man to reign over us.' When he returned, having received the kingly power, he commanded these servants, to whom he had given the money, to be called to him, that he might know what they had gained by trading.

The first came before him, saying, 'Lord, your pound has made ten pounds more.' And he said to him, 'Well done, good servant! Because you have been faithful in a very little, you shall have authority over ten cities.' And the second came, saying, 'Lord, your pound has made five pounds.' And he said to him, 'And you are to be over five cities.'

Then another came, saying, 'Lord, here is your pound, which I kept laid away in a napkin; for I was afraid of you, because you are a severe man; you take up what you did not lay down, and reap what you did not sow.' He said to him, 'I will condemn you out of your own mouth, you wicked servant! You knew that I was a severe man, taking up what I did not lay down and reaping what I did not sow? Why then did you not put my money into the bank, and at my coming I should have collected it with interest?' And he said to those who stood by, 'Take the pound from him, and give it to him who has the ten pounds.' (And they said to him, 'Lord, he has ten pounds!') 'I tell you, that to everyone who has will more be given; but from him who has not, even what he has will be taken away. But as for those enemies of mine, who did not want me to reign over them, bring them here and slay them before me.'

(L)

Do not lay up for yourselves treasures on earth,
where moth and rust consume
and where thieves break in and steal,

but lay up for yourselves treasures in heaven,
where neither moth nor rust consumes
and where thieves do not break in and steal.

For where your treasure is,
there will your heart be also.

(M — possibly Q)

If you are offering your gift
at the altar,
and there remember
that your brother has something against you,
leave your gift there
before the altar

and go
first be reconciled to your brother,
and then come
and offer your gift.

(M)

This poor widow*
has put in more than all of them;

for they all
out of their abundance
contributed,

but she
out of her poverty
put in all the living that she had.

(Mk)

---

*A poor widow observed in a crowd of those putting money into the offertory chest at the Jerusalem temple. Her two tiny coins were of more worth than the handsome sums contributed by others.

There was a rich man who had a steward, and charges were brought to him that this man was wasting his goods. And he called him and said to him, 'What is this that I hear about you? Turn in the account of your stewardship, for you can no longer be a steward.' And the steward said to himself, 'What shall I do, since my master is taking the stewardship away from me? I am not strong enough to dig, and I am ashamed to beg. I have decided what to do, so that people may receive me into their houses when I am put out of the stewardship.' So, summoning his master's debtors one by one, he said to the first, 'How much do you owe my master?' He said, 'A hundred measures of oil.' And he said to him, 'Take your bill, and sit down quickly and write fifty.' Then he said to another, 'And how much do you owe?' He said, 'A hundred measures of wheat.' He said to him, 'Take your bill, and write eighty.'

The master commended the dishonest steward for his prudence; for the sons of this world are wiser in their own generation than the sons of light.

And I tell you, make friends for yourselves by means of unrighteous mammon, so that, when it fails they may receive you into the eternal habitations.*

(L)

Who then is the faithful and wise steward,
whom his master will set over his household,
to give them their portion of food at the proper time?

Blessed is that servant
whom his master when he comes
will find so doing.

Truly I tell you,
he will set him
over all his possessions.

But if that servant says to himself,
'My master is delayed in coming,'
and begins to beat the menservants and the maidservants,
and to eat and drink and get drunk,

*The irony, and the humour contained in many of Jesus' sayings are so often missed that this parable has actually caused embarrassment, as if Jesus was seriously encouraging his hearers to swindle their employers and practise dishonesty!

the master of that servant
will come on a day when he does not expect him
and at an hour he does not know,

and will punish him,
and put him
with the unfaithful.

(Q)

The kings of the Gentiles
exercise lordship over them;
and those in authority over them
are called benefactors.
But not so
with you;

rather let the greatest among you
become as the youngest,
and the leader
as one who serves.

For which is the greater,
one who sits at table,
or one who serves?
Is it not the one who sits at table?

But I am among you
as one who serves.

(Mk)

In a certain city there was a judge who neither feared God nor regarded
man; and there was a widow in that city who kept coming to him
and saying, 'Vindicate me against my adversary.' For a while he refused;
but afterward he said to himself, 'Though I neither fear God nor regard
man, yet because this widow bothers me, I will vindicate her, or she
will wear me out by her continual coming.'

Hear what the unrighteous judge says. And will not God vindicate
his elect, who cry to him day and night? Will he delay long over
them? I tell you, he will vindicate them speedily. Nevertheless, when
the Son of man comes, will he find faith on earth?

(L)

A man had two sons;

and he went to the first
and said, 'Son, go and work in the vineyard today.'
And he answered,
'I will not';
but afterwards he repented and went.

And he went to the second
and said the same;
and he answered,
'I go, sir,'
but did not go.

Which of the two did the will of his father?

(M)

I tell you,

that to every one who has
will more be given;

but from him who has not
even what he has will be taken away.

(M & L)

Every one who divorces his wife
and marries another
commits adultery,

and he who marries a woman
divorced from her husband
commits adultery.

(Mk)

You, therefore, must be perfect,
as your heavenly Father is perfect.

(Q)

You have heard that it was said,
'You shall not commit adultery.'

But I say to you
that every one
who looks at a woman lustfully
has already
committed adultery with her in his heart.

(M)

No one after lighting a lamp puts it in a cellar or under a bushel,
but on a stand, that those who enter may see the light.

(Q)

The eye is the lamp of the body.

So, if your eye is sound,
your whole body will be full of light;
but if your eye is not sound,
your whole body will be full of darkness.

If then the light in you is darkness,
how great is the darkness!

(M—possibly Q)

Every one then who hears these words of mine
and does them
will be like a wise man
who built his house upon the rock;

and the rain fell, and the floods came,
and the winds blew and beat upon that house,

but it did not fall,
because it had been founded on the rock.

And every one who hears these words of mine
and does not do them
will be like a foolish man
who built his house upon the sand;

and the rain fell, and the floods came,
and the winds blew and beat against that house,

and it fell;
and great was the fall of it.

(M—possibly Q)

7

THE COST

THE Gospels contain two accounts of a period spent by Jesus in the desert in self-chosen solitude. It would seem that this was at the beginning of Jesus' three years or so of public ministry. During this retreat we are told that he was faced with various temptations, all of which he recognized and resisted. He then returned to society with an unstated but quite clear understanding of the way ahead.

The only possible source of information about this retreat and its temptations is Jesus himself. The temptations, poetically described, repay a good deal of meditation, but for our present purposes they may be briefly described as the easy, cheap ways of obtaining a following, the false ways of establishing the Kingdom. Recognizing them for what they were, Jesus was left with the only other way, that of total self-giving, without expectation of reward or even of return. In other words, the way of pure, unsentimental Love.

Jesus offered no cheap allurements. He dissuaded as often as he called. The cost of discipleship would be—not cheap, not expensive, but total.

He used every means to convey this simple, hard fact. He used the means of wild, poetic exaggeration. He used poems and parables, and he also spoke to his disciples directly, spelling out in a way unusual for him exactly what the cost would be for himself and, by implication, for them.

Jesus ran no 'bandwagon'. There were times when he was popular and there were times when he was not. The authorities, on the whole, distrusted, feared, and even hated him. Popularity and unpopularity came and went like the weather. Love demanded a response to the sufferings of men and women, and his healing ministry, always reluctantly exercised, was clamoured after. It was given because Love demanded it, but it was an exhausting distraction, that is clear. Over and over again he exhorted those whom he had healed to thank God and keep their mouths shut. They may have done the first, they seldom did the second and over and over again we find Jesus slipping away, avoiding the crowds, moving on to the next village, escaping to the hillsides away even from his closest disciples. The Prince of Peace was allowed no peace! A reading of the Gospels reveals him avoiding crowds as often as he encountered them. His was no triumphal progress.

The free gift of the self is the only expression of Love that there is. It is given in many ways and at many different levels as circumstances demand, but a man or a woman has nothing else to give. The self is itself *given* as a free gift by God. God is Love, the all-Giver. For the disciple of Jesus, therefore, there can be 'nothing in it for him or for her'. Love is its own reward. The gift of self is given only for the other, and for others.

No strings can be attached, no reservations can be made.

If any man would come after me,
let him deny himself
and take up his cross daily
and follow me.

For whoever would save his life
will lose it;
and whoever loses his life for my sake,
he will save it.

For what does it profit a man
if he gains the whole world
and loses or forfeits himself?

(Mk)

He who loves father or mother
more than me
is not worthy of me;

and he who loves son or daughter
more than me
is not worthy of me;

and he who does not take his cross
and follow me
is not worthy of me.

(Q)

Which of you, desiring to build a tower, does not first sit down and count the cost, whether he has enough to complete it? Otherwise, when he has laid a foundation, and is not able to finish, all who see it begin to mock him, saying, 'This man began to build, and was not able to finish.' Or what king, going to encounter another king in war, will not sit down first and take counsel whether he is able with ten thousand to meet him who comes against him with twenty thousand? And if not, while the other is a great way off, he sends an embassy and asks terms of peace. So therefore, whoever of you does not renounce all that he has cannot be my disciple.

(L)

Behold, I send you out as sheep
in the midst of wolves;
so be wise as serpents
and innocent as doves.

Beware of men;
for they will deliver you up
to councils,
and flog you
in their synagogues,

and you will be dragged
before governors and kings
for my sake
to bear testimony
before them and the Gentiles.

When they deliver you up,
do not be anxious
how or what you shall speak;*
for what you shall say
will be given to you in that hour.

For it is not you
who speak,
but the Spirit of your Father
speaking through you.

(Mk)

*The RSV text gives 'how *you are* to speak or what you are *to say*.' This is a paraphrase rather than a translation and upsets the balances of the verse (see note in *Poems of Jesus*, Vol. 1, p. 92).

Foxes
have holes,
and birds of the air
have nests;

but the Son of man
has nowhere to lay his head.

(Q)

He who hears you
hears me,
and he who rejects you
rejects me,
and he who rejects me
rejects him who sent me.

(Q)

The Son of man will be delivered into the hands of men, and they
will kill him; and when he is killed, after three days he will rise.

(Mk)

Truly, truly, I say to you,

unless a grain of wheat falls into the earth and dies
it remains alone;
but if it dies,
it bears much fruit.

He who loves his life
loses it,
and he who hates his life in this world
will keep it for eternal life.

(Mk and Jn)

Do not resist one who is evil.

But if any one strikes you
on the right cheek,
turn to him the other also;

and if any one would sue you
and take your coat,
let him have your cloak as well;

and if any one forces you
to go one mile,
go with him two miles.

(M—possibly Q)

What did you go out into the wilderness to behold?
A reed shaken by the wind?

Why then did you go out?
To see a man clothed in soft raiment?
Behold, those who wear soft raiment
are in kings' houses.

Why then did you go out?
To see a prophet?
Yes, I tell you,
and more than a prophet.*

This is he of whom it is written,
'Behold, I send my messenger before thy face,
'who shall prepare thy way before thee.'

(Q)

A servant is not greater than his master.

If they persecuted me,
they will also persecute you;
if they kept my word,
they will keep yours also.

(Jn)

Love your enemies,
do good to those who hate you,
bless those who curse you,
pray for those who abuse you.

(Q)

*John the Baptist.

Truly, I say to you,

among those born of women
there has risen no one greater than John the Baptist;
yet he who is least in the kingdom of heaven
is greater than he.

From the days of John the Baptist until now
the kingdom of heaven
has suffered violence,
and men of violence
take it by force.

For all the prophets and the law prophesied until John;*
and if you are willing to accept it,
he is Elijah who is to come.

He who has ears to hear
let him hear.

(M—possibly Q)

If any one serves me,
he must follow me;
and where I am,
there shall my servant be also;

if any one serves me,
the Father will honour him.

(Jn)

Truly, truly, I say to you,

You will weep and lament,
but the world will rejoice;
you will be sorrowful,
but your sorrow will turn into joy.

When a woman is in travail
she has sorrow,
because her hour has come;

*The cost to John the Baptist, for his discipleship, was unlawful
imprisonment, and being murdered in prison on the orders of a drunken
puppet-king anxious to impress important guests at a dinner-party.

but when she is delivered of the child,
she no longer remembers the anguish,
for joy that a child is born into the world.

So you have sorrow now,
but I will see you again
and your hearts will rejoice,
and no one will take your joy from you.

(Jn)

On that day, let him who is on the housetop, with his goods in the
house, not come down to take them away; and likewise let him who
is in the field not turn back. Remember Lot's wife. Whoever seeks
to gain his life will lose it, but whoever loses his life will preserve it.

(Q)

He who is greatest among you
shall be your servant;
whoever exalts himself
will be humbled,
and whoever humbles himself
will be exalted.

(M)

If the world hates you,
know that it hated me
before it hated you.

If you were of this world,
the world would love its own;

but because you are not of this world,
but I chose you out of the world,
therefore the world hates you.

(Jn)

And when they bring you before the synagogues and the rulers and
the authorities, do not be anxious how or what you are to answer
or what you are to say; for the Holy Spirit will teach you in that
very hour what you ought to say.

(Q)

Those whom I love,
I reprove and chasten;
so be zealous and repent.

(Revelation)

Now is my soul troubled.

And what shall I say?
'Father, save me from this hour?'

No,
for this purpose I have come to this hour.

Father, glorify thy name.

(Jn)

8

HEAVEN AND HELL

IT IS a commonplace that the ancient world conceived of a three-tier universe: Heaven, or the abode of God and his angels, the Underworld, or abode of the dead, and suspended between them this world of mortal men and women. This is of course an oversimplifcation, but it will serve for our present purpose.

Jesus was an inheritor of the Old Testament tradition which reflected this general pattern. To the Hebrews, Heaven was not considered accessible to mankind until quite late, and then only in apocalyptic speculation about Elijah, or mythological characters such as Enoch. *Sheol* (in Greek, Hades), the abode of the dead, was thought of as a vast cavern or pit beneath this world where rested the souls of the dead in, at best, a semi-conscious state, and very decidedly 'out of the action'. Necromancy, common, if not universal in the ancient world, was strictly forbidden among Hebrews.

Personal immortality was not a pressing concern until quite late in the tradition and then, very probably, through Babylonian or Greek influence. Under this same influence, speculation divided *Sheol* into two compartments: a favourable shadowland for the righteous, and a punitive shadowland for the wicked. In the very late Old Testament period, the punitive state was sometimes known as *Gehenna*. This word derived from *Ga-Hinnom,* a valley to the West of Jerusalem, the place of former pagan worship of a particularly barbarous nature, which had become the communal rubbish-tip. Refuse fires burned continually in the valley.

In this late period, in the speculation of the Pharisees, a hope developed of an eventual resurrection of the dead into a, presumably, non-physical life of God-related immortality. This hope was allied to the awaited *Day of the Lord* when the age dominated by Satan would come to an end and God's Kingship become universally manifest. There would be judgement on the wicked and vindication of the righteous. This eschatological hope, conceived in transcendental terms as 'other worldly' or at the very least 'trans-worldly', was linked with the looked-for *Messiah* who would represent God's intervention in human affairs.

Both in form and in vocabulary, the eschatology (teaching concerning the 'last things') of Jesus reflects the expectations of contemporary Judaism quite closely. There were no hard-and-fast credal formulae concerning these matters, indeed the Sadducee party, the 'Establishment', poured scorn on most of it; but in general terms, Jesus took the essential concepts for granted—the Day of the Lord, judgement and resurrection—and taught in those terms. He used the stark and alarming concept of *Gehenna* in a vivid and shocking way. He challenged his hearers with the image of the rubbish-dump, but his criteria were not at all those of contemporary ideas of 'righteousness'. The teaching of Jesus contained no crude theory of rewards and punishments, it served rather as the vehicle for conveying his fundamental religious and moral concepts. The shock of *Gehenna* was administered to Jesus' hearers and they were left to go away and think about it!

The main thrust of the teaching of Jesus is that the *Day of the Lord* has now dawned, that the 'Prince of this world' (Satan) is cast out, and that the Kingdom is already present and operative among men though awaiting its fullness and consummation.

A characteristic of the Kingdom is Eternal Life; the life of the coming age may be begun here and now, and the Kingdom and its Life transcend this mortal life. The consummation will be transcendental; indeed the Life of the Kingdom is transcendental by nature. Inherent in the Kingdom is a wholly new relationship between God and man. The *Marriage* of Heaven and earth, of God with his people, a concept which permeates much of the Old Testament, particularly in the writings of the Prophets, is even now in process of solemnization!

Enter by the narrow gate;

for the gate is wide
and the way is easy,
that leads to destruction,
and those who enter by it are many.

For the gate is narrow
and the way is hard,
that leads to life,
and those who find it are few.

(M)

The kingdom of heaven may be compared to a king
who wished to settle accounts with his servants.

When he began the reckoning,
one was brought to him
who owed him ten thousand talents;
and as he could not pay,
his lord ordered him to be sold, with his wife
and children and all that he had,
and payment to be made.

So the servant fell on his knees, imploring him,
'Lord, have patience with me,
'and I will pay you everything.'
And out of pity for him the lord of that servant
released him
and forgave him the debt.

But that servant, as he went out,
came upon one of his fellow-servants
who owed him a hundred denarrii;
and seizing him by the throat
he said,
'Pay what you owe.'

So his fellow servant fell down and besought him,
'Have patience with me,
'and I will pay you.'
He refused
and went and put him in prison
till he should pay the debt.

When his fellow servants saw what had taken place,
they were greatly distressed,
and they went and reported to their lord
all that had taken place.

Then his lord summoned him and said to him,
'You wicked servant!
'I forgave you all that debt
'because you besought me;
'and should not you
'have had mercy on your fellow servant
'as I
'had mercy on you ?'

And in anger his lord
delivered him to the jailers,
till he should pay all his debt.

So also my heavenly Father will do
to every one of you,
if you do not forgive
your brother from your heart.

(M)

I tell you, my friends, do not fear

those who kill the body,
and after that
have no more that they can do.

But I will warn you whom to fear;

Fear him who,
after he has killed,
has power to cast into hell;

yes, I tell you, fear him!

(Q)

Whoever is ashamed
of me and of my words,

of him
will the Son of man be ashamed
when he comes in his glory
and the glory of the Father and of the holy angels.

(Mk)

If your hand
causes you to sin,
cut it off;
it is better for you to enter life maimed
than with two hands
to go to hell,
to the unquenchable fire.

And if your foot
causes you to sin,
cut it off;
it is better for you to enter life lame
than with two feet
to be thrown into hell.

And if your eye
causes you to sin,
pluck it out;
it is better for you to enter the kingdom of God with one eye
than with two eyes
to be thrown into hell,
where their worm does not die,
and the fire is not quenched.

(Mk)

A man once gave a great banquet, and invited many; and at the time for the banquet he sent his servant to say to those who had been invited, 'Come; for all is now ready.' But they all alike began to make excuses. The first said to him, 'I have bought a field, and I must go out and see it; I pray you, have me excused.' And another said, 'I have bought five yoke of oxen, and I go to examine them; I pray you, have me excused.' And another said, 'I have married a wife, and therefore I cannot come.' So the servant came and reported this to his master.

Then the householder in anger said to his servant, 'Go out quickly to the streets and lanes of the city, and bring in the poor and maimed and blind and lame.' And the servant said, 'Sir, what you commanded has been done, and still there is room.' And the master said to the servant, 'Go out to the highways and hedges, and compel people to come in, that my house may be filled. For I tell you, none of those men who were invited shall taste my banquet.'

(Q)

When the Son of man comes in his glory,
and all the angels with him,
then will he sit on his glorious throne.
Before him will be gathered all the nations,

and he will separate them
one from another
as a shepherd separates
the sheep from the goats,

and he will place the sheep
at his right hand
but the goats
at the left.

Then the King will say to those at his right hand,

'Come, O blessed of my Father,
'inherit the kingdom
'prepared for you from the foundation of the world;

'for I was hungry and you gave me food,
'I was thirsty and you gave me drink,
'I was a stranger and you welcomed me,
'I was naked and you clothed me,
'I was sick and you visited me,
'I was in prison and you came to me.'

Then the righteous will answer him,

'Lord, when did we see thee hungry and feed thee,
'or thirsty and give thee drink?
'And when did we see thee a stranger and welcome thee,
'or naked and clothe thee?
'And when did we see thee sick or in prison and visit thee?'

And the King will answer them,

'Truly, I say to you,
'as you did it
'to one of the least of these my brethren,
'you did it
'to me.'

Then he will say to those at his left hand,

'Depart from me, you cursed,
'into the eternal fire
'prepared for the devil and his angels;

'for I was hungry and you gave me no food,
'I was thirsty and you gave me no drink,
'I was a stranger and you did not welcome me,
'naked and you did not clothe me,
'sick and in prison, and you did not visit me.'

Then they also will answer,

'Lord, when did we see thee hungry or thirsty
'or a stranger or naked
'or sick or in prison,
'and did not minister to thee?'

Then he will answer them,

'Truly, I say to you,
'as you did it not
'to one of the least of these,
'you did it not
'to me.'

And they will go away
into eternal punishment,
but the righteous
into eternal life.

(M)

Truly, truly, I say to you,
the hour is coming, and now is,

when the dead
will hear the voice of the Son of God,
and those who hear
will live.

For as the Father
has life in himself,
so he has granted the Son also
to have life in himself,

and has given him authority to execute judgement,
because he is the Son of man.

Do not marvel at this;
for the hour is coming

when all who are in the tombs
will hear his voice and come forth,

those who have done good,
to the resurrection of life,
and those who have done evil,
to the resurrection of judgement.

(Jn)

Every one who is angry with his brother
shall be liable to judgement;
whoever insults his brother
shall be liable to the council,
and whoever says, 'You fool!'
shall be liable to the hell of fire.

(M)

There were many widows in Israel
in the days of Elijah,
when the heaven was shut up three years and six months,
when there came a great famine over all the land;
and Elijah was sent to none of them
but only to Zarephath, in the land of Sidon,
to a woman who was a widow.

And there were many lepers in Israel
in the time of the prophet Elisha;
and none of them was cleansed,
but only Naaman the Syrian.

(L)

As it was in the days of Noah,
so will it be in the days of the Son of man;
they ate, they drank,
they married, they were given in marriage,
until the day when Noah entered the ark,
and the flood came and destroyed them all.

Likewise as it was in the days of Lot—
they ate, they drank,
they bought, they sold,
they planted, they built,
but on the day when Lot went out from Sodom
fire and brimstone rained from heaven and destroyed them
    all—

So will it be when the Son of man is revealed.

                                                        (Q)

Can the wedding guests fast
while the bridegroom is with them?
As long as they have the bridegroom with them,
they cannot fast.

The days will come,
when the bridegroom is taken away from them,
and then they will fast
in that day.

                                                        (Mk)

Strive to enter by the narrow door;
for many, I tell you, will seek to enter
and will not be able.

When once the householder has risen up
and shut the door,
you will begin to stand outside
and to knock at the door,

saying,
'Lord, open to us.'

He will answer you,
'I do not know where you come from.'

Then you will begin to say,
'We ate and drank in your presence,
'and you taught in our streets.'

But he will say,
'I tell you, I do not know where you come from;
'depart from me, all you workers of iniquity!'

(Q)

When you see a cloud rising in the west,

you say at once,
'A shower is coming';
and so it happens.

And when you see the south wind blowing,
you say,
'There will be scorching heat';
and it happens.

You hypocrites! You know how to interpret
the appearance of earth and sky;
but why do you not know how to interpret
the present time?

(Q)

Not every one who says to me, 'Lord, Lord,'
shall enter the kingdom of heaven,
but he who does the will of my Father who is in heaven.

On that day many will say to me, 'Lord, Lord,'
'did we not prophesy in your name,
'and cast out demons in your name,
'and do many mighty works in your name?'

And then I will declare to them, 'I never knew you;
'depart from me,
'you evildoers.'

(M)

If I had not come
and spoken to them,
they would not have sin;
but now
they have no excuse
for their sin.

He who hates me
hates my Father also.

If I had not done among them
the works which no one else did,
they would not have sin;
but now
they have seen and hated
both me and my Father.

It is to fulfil the word that is written in their law,
'They hated me without a cause.'

(Jn)

Every one who acknowledges me before men,
I also will acknowledge before my Father who is in heaven;
but whoever denies me before men,
I also will deny before my Father who is in heaven.

(Q)

Do you think that these Galilaeans were worse sinners
than all the other Galilaans,
because they suffered thus?

I tell you, No;
but unless you repent
you will all likewise perish.

Or those eighteen upon whom the tower in Siloam fell and
    killed them
do you think that they were worse offenders
than all the others who dwelt in Jerusalem?

I tell you, No;
but unless you repent
you will all likewise perish.*

(L)

There you will weep and gnash your teeth, when you see Abraham
and Isaac and Jacob and all the prophets in the kingdom of God and
you yourselves thrust out. And men will come from east and west,
and from north and south, and sit at table in the kingdom of God.
And behold, some are last who will be first, and some are first who
will be last.

(Q)

Daughters of Jerusalem,
do not weep for me,
but weep for yourselves
and for your children.

For behold the days are coming
when they will say,
'Blessed are the barren,
'and the wombs that never bore,
'and the breasts that never gave suck!'

Then they will begin to say
to the mountains, 'Fall on us';
and to the hills, 'Cover us.'

For if they do this when the wood is green,
what will happen when it is dry?

(L)

In that night

there will be two men in one bed;
one will be taken
and the other left.

*A reference to the naïve idea that victims of political or natural catastrophe
must have been sinners and were thus 'punished' for their sinfulness.

There will be two women grinding together;
one will be taken
and the other left.

(Q)

Blessed are your eyes,
for they see,
and your ears,
for they hear.

Truly, I say to you,
many prophets and righteous men

longed to see
what you see,
and did not see it,

and to hear
what you hear,
and did not hear it.

(Q)

9

FAITH AND
THE CHURCH

THE old English word 'Belief' (which is akin to *lief* and *love*) has given place to a Latin/French word, 'Faith'. Faith has become a loaded word, carrying a great weight of technical, theological meaning, all of it developed after the lifetime of Jesus, though largely in response to man's experience of him. We therefore need to look at the Old Testament which provided the vocabulary of Jesus, and his thought-forms, in order to discover what Faith, or Belief, meant to him.

Here again we must beware, because, with the adoption of the word Faith, the word Belief has become attached to intellectual assent, Faith being reserved for ethical, religious assent. This distinction, met with in other books of the New Testament is not present in the Old. 'You believe that God is one,' says St James, 'you do well. Even the demons believe—and shudder!' The object of Faith is God. Philosophical opinionation is quite foreign to the Old Testament *milieu*.

Faith, or Belief, is met with twice only in the Old Testament. Its first use, in Deuteronomy, signifies steadfastness and fidelity. It is a passive rather than an active use. The second, in the prophecy of Habakkuk, is of a different character. Here the context suggests an active meaning. Steadfastness is manifest in steadfast adherence. Passive fidelity has become active Faith.

Neither the Old Testament nor the New wastes time arguing for the existence of God. Belief in the God revealed by the Scriptures is taken for granted. It is only the fool who says in his heart, 'There is no God!' Faith, or Belief, as understood by Jesus is an active, trusting, and steadfast response to a *person*. Jesus challenged his hearers to Faith in himself. He, bearing the *persona* which he steadfastly refused to define, is the object of Faith, all within the overall context of Faith in the God which the Old Testament reveals. Jesus did not invite theological or philosophical speculation as to the nature of his *persona*; he cared nothing for opinion in such matters. He simply challenged his hearers to have Faith in him, to Believe.

The word which, in English, is translated 'Church' is the Greek word *ekklesia*. In secular Greek it was used to describe an assembly of citizens of a self-governing city, and this usage is met with in the New Testament to describe the assembly at Ephesus. In the Greek-language version of the Old Testament known as the Septuagint—in almost universal use among Jews outside Palestine and quoted almost exclusively in the New Testament—*ekklesia* means the 'congregation' or more broadly, those 'within the covenant'. It is clear that this word was in regular use very early on in the New Testament period to describe the Christian congregation in the Greek-speaking world. The extent to which this word may have been 'borrowed' in popular Palestinian use is unknown to us, as is the Aramaic equivalent.

Jesus is reported as referring to the Church twice only and both of these occasions are found in the Gospel according to St Matthew. Both are consistent with the usage in the Septuagint, and with the usage of the very early Christian community.

The word 'Church' is found elsewhere in the New Testament to describe states of affairs *after* the life of Jesus, and it is part of the response of men to the Jesus-experience. It quickly became the word used to describe the community of those who had put their faith in Jesus, the communiy of those within the New Covenant which he proclaimed. This has been its meaning ever since.

A question remains unanswered, however. Are the Church and the Kingdom one and the same? This question has puzzled Christian thinkers for nearly two thousand years. Whatever the answer is, it appears to be neither a simple 'yes' nor a simple 'no'.

I am the resurrection and the life;

he who believes in me,
though he die,
yet shall he live,

and whoever lives
and believes in me
shall never die.

(Jn)

This is the work of God, that you believe in him whom he has sent.

(Jn)

You are from below,
I am from above;
You are of this world,
I am not of this world.

I told you
that you would die in your sins,
for unless you believe that I am he,
you will die in your sins.

(Jn)

He who believes in me,
believes not in me
but in him who sent me.

And he who sees me,
sees him who sent me.

(Jn)

Do you now believe? The hour is coming, indeed it has come, when
you will be scattered, every man to his home, and will leave me alone;
yet I am not alone, for the Father is with me. I have said to you,
that in me you may have peace. In the world you have tribulation;
but be of good cheer, I have overcome the world.

(Jn)

Truly, truly, I say to you,

We speak
of what we know,
and bear witness
to what we have seen;
but you do not receive
our testimony.

If I have told you earthly things
and you do not believe,
how can you believe
if I tell you heavenly things.

(Jn)

Truly, truly, I say to you,

he who believes in me,
will also do
the works that I do;

and greater works than these
will he do,
because I go to the Father.

(Jn)

Have you believed because you have seen me? Blessed are those who
have not seen and yet believe.

(Jn)

All that the Father gives me
will come to me;
and him who comes to me
I will not cast out.

For I have come down from heaven,
not to do my own will,
but the will of him who sent me;

and this is the will of him who sent me,
that I should lose nothing
of all that he has given me,
but raise it up at the last day.

For this is the will of my Father,
that every one who sees the Son
and believes in him
should have eternal life;
and I will raise him up at the last day.

(Jn)

You are the light of the world. A city set on a hill cannot be hid.
Nor do men light a lamp and put it under a bushel, but on a stand,
and it gives light to all in the house. Let your light so shine before
men, that they may see your good works and give glory to your Father
who is in heaven.

(M)

You are those
who have continued with me in my trials;

as my Father appointed a kingdom
for me,
so do I appoint
for you

that you may eat and drink at my table
in my kingdom,
and sit on thrones
judging the twelve tribes of Israel.

(L)

If a man loves me.
he will keep my word,

and my Father will love him
and we will come to him
and make our home with him.

He who does not love me
does not keep my words;

and the word which you hear
is not mine
but the Father's who sent me.

(Jn)

And no one tears a piece
from a new garment
and puts it
upon an old garment;

if he does
he will tear the new,
and the piece from the new
will not match the old.

And no one puts new wine
into old wineskins;

if he does,
the new wine
will burst the skins
and it will be spilled,
and the skins will be destroyed.

But new wine must be put
into fresh wineskins.

(Mk)

A disciple is not above his teacher,
nor a servant above his master;
it is enough for the disciple to be like his teacher,
and the servant like his master.

If they have called the master of the house Beelzebul,
how much more will they malign those of his household.

(M)

The light is with you for a little longer.

Walk while you have the light,
lest the darkness overtake you;
he who walks in the darkness
does not know where he goes.

While you have the light,
believe in the light,
that you may become sons of light.

(Jn)

He who has my commandments
and keeps them,
he it is who loves me;
and he who loves me
will be loved by my Father,
and I will love him
and manifest myself to him.

(Jn)

Go and tell John what you hear and see;*

The blind receive their sight
and the lame walk,
lepers are cleansed
and the deaf hear,
and the dead are raised up,
and the poor have good news preached to them.

And blessed is he
who takes no offence at me.

(Q)

Behold,
I stand at the door
and knock;
if any one hears my voice
and opens the door,
I will come in to him
and eat with him,
and he with me.

(Revelation)

I am the true vine,
and my Father is the vinedresser.

Every branch of mine
that bears no fruit,
he takes away,

and every branch
that does bear fruit
he prunes**
that it may bear more fruit.

You are already made clean†
by the word which I have spoken to you.

---

*A message of reassurance to John the Baptist in prison.
**The Greek = literally, 'cleanses'.
†The Greek = literally, 'pruned'.

Abide in me,
and I in you.

As the branch cannot bear fruit by itself,
unless it abide in the vine,
neither can you,
unless you abide in me.

I am the vine,
you are the branches.

He who abides in me,
and I in him,
he it is that bears much fruit,
for apart from me
you can do nothing.

If a man does not abide in me,
he is cast forth as a branch
and withers;
and the branches are gathered,
thrown into the fire
and burned.

If you abide in me,
and my words abide in you,

ask whatever you will,
and it shall be done for you.

By this my Father is glorified,
that you bear much fruit,
and so prove to be my disciples.

(Jn)

Blessed are you, Simon Bar-Jonah!*
For flesh and blood has not revealed this to you,
but my Father who is in heaven.

*The Apostle Peter (Petrus = Latin for 'Rock', Greek = Cephas, a
nickname). Peter had proclaimed belief that Jesus was 'The Christ, the Son
of the living God'.

And I tell you,
you are Peter,
and on this rock
I will build my church,
and the powers of death shall not prevail against it.

I will give you the keys of the kingdom of heaven,
and whatever you bind on earth,
shall be bound in heaven,
and whatever you loose on earth,
shall be loosed in heaven.

(M)

Truly, truly, I say to you,

unless one is born of water and the Spirit,
he cannot enter the kingdom of God.

That which is born of the flesh
is flesh,
and that which is born of the Spirit
is Spirit.

Do not marvel that I said to you,
'You must be born anew.'

The wind blows where it wills,
and you hear the sound of it,
but you do not know
whence it comes
or whither it goes;

So it is with every one
who is born of the Spirit.

(Jn)

All authority in heaven and on earth has been given to me. Go therefore
and make disciples of all nations, baptizing them in the name of the
Father and of the Son and of the Holy Spirit, teaching them to observe
all that I have commanded you; and lo, I am with you always, to the
close of the age.

(M)

You will know
the truth,
and the truth
will make you free.

(Jn)

Truly, truly, I say to you,

if you ask anything of the Father
he will give it you
in my name.

Hitherto you have asked nothing
in my name;

ask,
and you will receive,
that your joy may be full.

(Jn)

You are the salt of the earth; but if salt has lost its taste, how shall
its saltness be restored? It is no longer good for anything except to
be thrown out and trodden under foot by men.

(M)

Ask,
and it will be given you;
seek,
and you will find;
knock,
and it will be opened to you.

For everyone who asks
receives,
and he who seeks
finds,
and to him who knocks
it will be opened.

(M—possibly Q)

Whatever you ask
in my name,
I will do it,

that the Father
may be glorified
in the Son;

if you ask anything
in my name,
I will do it.

(Jn)

What man of you,

if his son asks him for bread,
will give him a stone?
or if he asks for a fish,
will give him a serpent?

If you then, who are evil,
know how to give good gifts
to your children,

How much more will your Father who is in heaven
give good things
to those who ask him!

(Q)

A new commandment I give to you,
that you love one another;

even as I have loved you,
that you also love one another.

By this all men will know that you are my disciples,
if you have love for one another.

(Jn)

If you had faith as a grain of mustard seed, you could say to this sycamine
tree, 'Be rooted up, and be planted in the sea,' and it would obey you.

(Q)

Blessed are you poor,
for yours is the kingdom of God.
Blessed are you that hunger now,
for you shall be satisfied.
Blessed are you that weep now,
for you shall laugh.
Blessed are you when men hate you,

and when they exclude you
and revile you,
and cast out your name as evil,
on account of the Son of man!
Rejoice in that day,
and leap for joy,
for behold, your reward is great in heaven.

But woe to you that are rich,
for you have received your consolation.
Woe to you that are full now,
for you shall hunger.
Woe to you that laugh now,
for you shall mourn and weep.
Woe to you, when all men speak well of you,
for so their fathers did to the false prophets.

(Q)

Peace I leave with you;
my peace I give to you;

not as the world gives
do I give to you.

(Jn)

A sower went out to sow his seed;
and as he sowed,

some fell along the path,
and was trodden underfoot,
and the birds of the air devoured it.

And some fell on the rock;
and as it grew up,
it withered away because it had no moisture.

And some fell among thorns;
and the thorns grew with it
and choked it.

And some fell into good soil
and grew,
and yielded a hundredfold.

(Mk)

Whatever house you enter,
first say, 'Peace be to this house!'

And if a son of peace is there,
your peace shall rest upon him;
but if not,
it shall return to you.

And remain in the same house,
eating and drinking what they provide,
for the labourer deserves his wages;
do not go from house to house.

Whenever you enter a town
and they receive you,

eat what is set before you;
heal the sick in it

and say to them,
'The kingdom of God has come near to you.'

But whenever you enter a town
and they do not receive you,

go into its streets and say,
'Even the dust of your town that clings to our feet,
'we wipe off against you;

'nevertheless know this,
'that the kingdom of God has come near.'

I tell you,
it shall be more tolerable on that day for Sodom
than for that town.

(Q)

I have other sheep,
that are not of this fold;
I must bring them also,
and they will heed my voice.

So there shall be one flock,
one shepherd.

(Jn)

The harvest is plentiful,
but the labourers are few;
pray therefore the Lord of the harvest
to send out labourers into his harvest.

(Q)

These things I have spoken to you while I am still with you. But
the Counsellor, the Holy Spirit, whom the Father will send in my
name, he will teach you all things, and bring to your remembrance
all that I have said to you.

(Jn)

It is to your advantage that I go away,
for if I do not go away,
the Counsellor will not come to you;
but if I go,
I will send him to you.

And when he comes
he will convince the world
of sin
and of righteousness
and of judgement:

of sin
because they do not believe in me;
of righteousness,
because I go to the Father,
and you see me no more;
of judgement,
because the ruler of this world is judged.

(Jn)

I have said this to you in figures; the hour is coming when I shall no longer speak to you in figures but tell you plainly of the Father. In that day you will ask in my name; and I do not say to you that I shall pray the Father for you; for the Father himself loves you, because you have loved me and have believed that I came from the Father.

(Jn)

In praying do not heap up empty phrases as the Gentiles do; for they think that they will be heard for their many words. Do not be like them, for your Father knows what you need before you ask him. Pray then like this:

> Our Father who art in heaven,
> Hallowed be thy name.
> Thy kingdom come
> Thy will be done,
> On earth as it is in heaven.
> Give us this day our daily bread;
> And forgive us our debts,
> As we also have forgiven our debtors;
> And lead us not into temptation,
> But deliver us from evil.

(M)

For I received from the Lord what I also delivered to you, that the Lord Jesus on the night when he was betrayed took bread, and when he had given thanks, he broke it, and said, 'This is my body which is for you. Do this in remembrance of me.' In the same way also the cup, after supper, saying, 'This cup is the new covenant in my blood. Do this, as often as you drink it, in remembrance of me.'

(St Paul, writing to the Church in Corinth)

Drink of it, all of you; for this is my blood of the covenant, which is poured out for many for the forgiveness of sins. I tell you I shall not drink again of this fruit of the vine until that day when I drink it new with you in my Father's kingdom.

(Mk and M)

Peace be with you.

As the Father
has sent me,
even so I
send you.

(Jn)

10

JUDGEMENT

THE unique character of the developing religion of the Old Testament was its very early recognition of the fact that religion and human conduct are inextricably bound up one with the other. This is a commonplace to us but was by no means a commonplace to the ancient world. The God of Israel is a *Person*, indeed He is Person itself, the source of all persons. He is knowable by man, made in his image, in personal terms. This is indeed the only way by which He can be known. He cannot, by any stretch of the imagination, be 'known about'.

The relationship between God and His people is personal, corporately and also individually. The Covenant, or relationship between God and Israel (i.e. 'people of God') is to be understood in inter-personal, that is to say *moral,* terms. It is enshrined in a code of human behaviour, both man to God, and man to his fellow men. In the earlier years of the Old Testament period, it was the corporate relationship that was paramount. The individual stood or fell by his being part of the corporate whole of Israel.

Before the Exile in the sixth century BC it is probably true to say that the God of Israel was understood as a tribal deity with territorial limits, competing with other tribal deities. The realization that the God of Israel was the Creator of Heaven and Earth began to dawn before the Exile, and to colour the vision of the various editors of the Scriptures, but it was the experience of the Exile which brought home to Israel the universal significance of her history and her vocation.

The theme of judgement runs throughout the Old Testament and into the New. God is judge. There is a consequence built into every action, man will 'get away with' nothing. The problem of the sufferings of the innocent exercised the Old Testament thinkers all the time. Suffering is a consequence of sin; the evil may prosper but their misdeeds will catch up with them. The righteous will be vindicated. God is judge and God is just. However much this might seem to fly in the face of day-to-day experience, the belief is axiomatic.

The whole history of Israel is seen in terms of God's judgement.

Her calamities are a direct consequence of her infidelities. References in the Old Testament to fornication and adultery refer, not to individual moral lapses, but to the corporate moral lapses of Israel in infidelity to her Lover, her Husband, her Master, her God. This is, for the most part, their New Testament reference as well.

God is the Creator of all things and thus the whole creation comes under His judgement. Its integrity depends upon its fidelity to His purpose. Mankind has sinned, humanity has lost its integrity, as the myth of Adam and Eve seeks to explain, giving expression to a state of affairs of universal experience. But it is not only Israel that is under judgement; the heathen world is equally under judgement and equally usable by God for the fulfilment of His purposes, often as instruments of punishment upon His unfaithful Israel. The experience of the Exile revealed to some, if not to others in Israel, that God's judgement—which is inseparable from His Compassion and His mercy—extends to all mankind. The vision of the writer of the second half of Isaiah is decidedly universalist.

This is the ambience into which Jesus was born and he affirmed the reality of judgement immediately, but turned the prevailing criteria upside down. Within the context of a Judaism turned inward and exclusivist, increasingly concerned with observance and a kind of 'legal righteousness', Jesus was totally universalist. The totality of mankind was his concern, however restrictedly Judaism was his context.

God's judgement would be revealed against his own people for setting aside the laws of God and relying on man-made rules and regulation, for the falseness of their criteria, above all for failing to recognize and to respond to the moment of Truth, the fulfilment of their history, the consummation of their whole vocation in the person and *persona* of Jesus himself. But built into this very prophecy of judgement is a poignant awareness of its inevitability; man is a sinner, and this is the whole point, and at the same time the tragedy, both of Israel and of Jesus himself, the 'Hope of Israel'.

The Fourth Gospel proclaims God's judgement upon 'the world'; the whole world of false values, false criteria, unreality and make-believe which is to be set starkly against 'the Kingdom'. The contrast is between lost integrity and integrity restored, and judgement, while described in courtroom images, is built in to every action and every circumstance, the sole criterion being fidelity to the loving purposes of God and to His Truth.

For judgement I came into this world,

that those who do not see
may see,
and that those who see
may become blind.

(Jn)

The Father

judges no one,
but has given all judgement
to the Son,

that all may honour the Son,
even as they honour the Father.
He who does not honour the Son
does not honour the Father who sent him.

(Jn)

If any one hears my sayings
and does not keep them,
I do not judge him
for I did not come
to judge the world
but to save the world.

He who rejects me
and does not receive my sayings
has a judge;
the word that I have spoken
will be his judge
on the last day.

For I have not spoken
on my own authority;
the Father who sent me
has himself given me commandment
what to say
and what to speak.

And I know that his commandment is eternal life.
What I say, therefore,
I say as the Father has bidden me.

(Jn)

Nothing is covered up
that will not be revealed,
or hidden
that will not be known.

Whatever you have said in the dark
shall be heard in the light,
and what you have whispered in private rooms
shall be proclaimed upon the housetops.

(Q)

God sent the Son into the world,
not to condemn the world,
but that the world might be saved
through him.

He who believes in him
is not condemned;

he who does not believe
is condemned already,
because he has not believed
in the name of the only Son of God.

And this is the judgement,
that the light has come into the world,
and men loved darkness rather than light,
because their deeds were evil.

For every one who does evil
hates the light,
and does not come to the light,
lest his deeds should be exposed.

But he who does what is true
comes to the light,
that it may be clearly seen
that his deeds have been wrought in God.

(Jn)

The land of a rich man brought forth plentifully; and he thought to himself, 'What shall I do, for I have nowhere to store my crops?' And he said, 'I will do this; I will pull down my barns, and build larger ones; and there I will store all my grain and my goods. And I will say to my soul, Soul, you have ample goods laid up for many years; take your ease, eat, drink, be merry.' But God said to him, 'Fool! This night your soul is required of you; and the things you have prepared, whose will they be? So is he who lays up treasure for himself and is not rich toward God.

(L)

That servant who knew his master's will,
but did not make ready
or act according to his will,
shall receive a severe beating.

But he who did not know,
and did what deserved a beating,
shall receive a light beating.

(Q)

Even if I do bear witness to myself,
my testimony is true,

for I know
whence I have come
and whither I am going,

but you do not know
whence I come
or whither I am going.

You judge according to the flesh,
I judge no one.
Yet even if I do judge,
my judgement is true,
for it is not I alone who judge,
but I and he who sent me.

In your law it is written
that the testimony of two men is true;

I bear witness to myself,
and the Father who sent me
bears witness to me.

(Jn)

Judge not,
and you will not be judged;
condemn not,
and you will not be condemned;
forgive,
and you will be forgiven;

give
and it will be given to you;
good measure, pressed down, shaken together, running over,
will be put into your lap.
For the measure you give
will be the measure you get back.

(Q)

Do not think that I
shall accuse you to the Father;
it is Moses
who accuses you,
on whom
you set your hope.

If you believed Moses
you would believe me,
for he
wrote of me.

But if you do not believe
his writings,
how will you believe
my words?

(Jn)

Temptations to sin are sure to come; but woe to him by whom they
come! It would be better for him if a millstone were hung round his
neck and he were cast into the sea, than that he should cause one
of these little ones to sin.

(Q)

He who receives a prophet
because he is a prophet
shall receive a prophet's reward,

and he who receives a righteous man
because he is a righteous man
shall receive a righteous man's reward.

And whoever gives to one of these little ones
even a cup of cold water
because he is a disciple,

truly, I say to you,
he shall not lose his reward.

(M)

I can do nothing on my own authority;
as I hear
I judge;
and my judgement
is just.

Because I seek
not my own will
but the will of him who sent me.

(Jn)

For no good tree
bears bad fruit,
nor again does a bad tree
bear good fruit;

for each tree
is known by its own fruit.

For figs are not gathered
from thorns,
nor are grapes picked
from a bramble bush.

The good man
out of the good treasure of his heart
produces good,

and the evil man
out of his evil treasure
produces evil;

for out of the abundance of the heart
his mouth speaks.

(Q)

Woe to you, Chorazin!
woe to you, Bethsaida!

for if the mighty works done in you
had been done in Tyre and Sidon,
they would have repented long ago in sackcloth and ashes.

But I tell you,
it shall be more tolerable
on the day of judgement
for Tyre and Sidon
than for you.

And you, Capernaum,
will you be exalted to heaven?
You shall be brought down to Hades.

For if the mighty works done in you
had been done in Sodom,
it would have remained until this day.

But I tell you
that it shall be more tolerable
on the day of judgement
for the land of Sodom
than for you.

(Q)

The men of Niniveh will arise
at the judgement
with this generation
and condemn it;

for they repented
at the preaching of Jonah,
and behold, something greater than Jonah is here.

The queen of the South will arise
at the judgement
with this generation
and condemn it;

for she came from the ends of the earth
to hear the wisdom of Solomon,
and behold, something greater than Solomon is here.

(Q)

A man had a fig tree planted in his vineyard; and he came seeking
fruit on it and found none. And he said to the vinedresser, 'Lo, these
three years I have come seeking fruit on this fig tree, and I find none.
Cut it down; why should it use up the ground?' And he answered
him, 'Let it alone, sir, this year also, till I dig about it and put on
manure. And if it bears fruit next year, well and good; but if not,
you can cut it down.'

(L)

*The following is a carefully constructed prophetic denunciation of quite alarming
force. The 'Scribes and Pharisees' who are the subject of unreserved condemnation
represent a tendency, an attitude of mind, inherent in all forms of 'established'
and institutionalized religion. Man-made religion has stifled God's Truth; outward
appearances, formal observances, smug self-righteousness have turned 'religion'
into a god. No Christian of any denominational persuasion can read what
follows without a sense of exceeding unease.*

Woe to you, scribes and Pharisees, hypocrites!
because you shut the kingdom of heaven against men;
for you neither enter yourselves,
nor allow who would enter to go in.

Woe to you, scribes and Pharisees, hypocrites!
For you travel sea and land to make a simple proselyte,
and when he becomes a proselyte,*
you make him twice as much a child of hell as yourselves.

*proselyte—a non-Jewish convert to the Jewish religion.

Woe to you, blind guides,
who say,
'If any one swears by the temple,
'it is nothing;
'but if any one swears by the gold of the temple,
'he is bound by his oath.'
You blind fools!
For which is greater, the gold
or the temple that has made the gold sacred?

And you say,
'If any one swears by the altar,
'it is nothing;
'but if any one swears by the gift that is on the altar,
'he is bound by his oath.'
You blind men!
For which is greater, the gift
or the altar that makes the gift sacred?

So he who swears by the altar,
swears by it
and by everything on it;
and he who swears by the temple,
swears by it
and by him who dwells in it;

and he who swears by heaven,
swears by the throne of God
and by him who sits upon it.

Woe to you, scribes and Pharisees, hypocrites!
for you tythe
mint and dill and cummin,
and have neglected
the weightier matters of the law,
justice, mercy and faith;

these you ought to have done,
without neglecting the others.

You blind guides,
straining out a gnat,
and swallowing a camel!

Woe to you, scribes and Pharisees, hypocrites!
for you cleanse the outside of the cup and of the plate,
but inside they are full of extortion and rapacity.

You blind Pharisee!
First cleanse the inside of the cup and of the plate,
that the outside also may be clean.

Woe to you, scribes and Pharisees, hypocrites!
for you are like whitewashed tombs,
which outwardly appear beautiful
but within they are full of dead men's bones and all
　　uncleanness.

So you also
outwardly appear righteous to men,
but within are full of hypocrisy and iniquity.

Woe to you, scribes and Pharisees, hypocrites!
for you build the tombs of the prophets
and adorn the monuments of the righteous,
saying,
'If we have lived
'in the days of our fathers,
'we would not have taken part
'with them in shedding the blood of the prophets.'

Thus you witness against yourselves,
that you are the sons of those who murdered the prophets.
Fill up, then,
the measure of your fathers.

You serpents,
you brood of vipers,
how are you to escape
being sentenced to hell?

　　　　　　　　　　　　　　　　(M—fragments in Q)

11

ETERNAL LIFE

THROUGHOUT the greater part of the Old Testament, the idea of a future life is conspicuous by its absence; indeed there are passages which seem specifically to deny it. This world alone is 'the land of the living' and although the hope of a 'life of the age to come' grew as the Old Testament period drew to its close, it could possibly be argued that 're-absorption' was the most widespread best post-mortem hope of the period.

The Apocryphal books present us with some speculations about a life after this one, but in general the tone is the same as in the bulk of the Canonical literature. Life is a blessing from God, death is a curse. Life is a 'loan which can be recalled'.

Jesus did not invent the concept of *Eternal Life*; it was in the Rabbinic vocabulary already, and many of Jesus' expressions were common Rabbinic ones. However, in stark contrast to anything that had happened before, Jesus presented Eternal Life as the chief topic of his teaching. Here it must be said that the *Kingdom,* to which the Synoptic tradition bears testimony, and *Eternal Life,* the main burden of the Johannine tradition, are totally interrelated. Eternal Life belongs to the Kingdom; it is a consequence of membership of it.

The life of the Kingdom is not to be understood as being merely of endless duration (time and duration are misleading concepts when man attempts the impossible and tries to think about Eternity). The life of the Kingdom is the *fullness of all life.* It is made clear throughout the Gospels that *belief* is the key to it and Jesus himself the mediator of it. Belief in, acceptance of, the person and *persona* of Jesus is the way of entry into the Kingdom and its Eternal Life. This is to be understood as a participation in God's eternal being—one might almost say 'a new contract of existence' for mankind.

Concerning this mortal life; the mournfulness of much of the Old Testament as to its brevity and its trials is wholly absent from Jesus. He exhibits genuine *joie de vivre* and is criticized for it. Over-anxiety concerning this life and its goods is sharply criticized; detachment, simplicity and the sacredness of all life are central to Jesus' teaching. He does not moralize, *he lives,* and it is significant that St John observed of him that, 'in him was life'.

Jesus proclaims a new and transcendental order of existence, and a transcendental life of which the Kingdom and its life are the manifestation among mortal men. The Hebrew language, and Aramaic, do not lend themselves to philosophical discussion, but Jesus was no philosopher. He was no theologian either, in the modern, Western meaning of the word. Jesus did not speculate or philosophize; *he proclaimed,* with all the vividness and vigour at his command. And it may be observed that the Resurrection and his post-Resurrection teachings and actions are, among other things, a wholly consistent *demonstration* of the Reality which he unswervingly proclaimed throughout his teaching ministry.

Yet a little while,

and the world will see me no more,
but you will see me;

because I live,
you will live also.

(Jn)

As the Father has loved me,
so have I loved you;
abide in my love.

If you keep my commandments,
you will abide in my love,
just as I have kept my Father's commandments
and abide in his love.

(Jn)

Let not your hearts be troubled;
believe in God,
believe also in me.

In my Father's house are many rooms;
if it were not so, would I have told you
that I go
to prepare a place for you?

and when I go
and prepare a place for you,
I will come again
and will take you to myself,

that where I am
you may be also.

(Jn)

Truly, truly, I say to you,

he who believes
has eternal life.

I am the bread of life.
Your fathers ate the manna in the wilderness,
and they died.

This is the bread which comes down from heaven;
that a man may eat of it
and not die.

I am the living bread which came down from
    heaven;
if any one eats of this bread,
he will live for ever;

and the bread which I give
is my flesh,
for the life of the world.

(Jn)

I am the bread of life;
he who comes to me
shall not hunger,
and he who believes in me
shall never thirst.

(Jn)

Truly, truly, I say to you,

unless you eat the flesh of the Son of man
and drink his blood,
you have no life in you;

he who eats my flesh
and drinks my blood
has eternal life,
and I will raise him up at the last day.

For my flesh is food indeed
and my blood is drink indeed.

(Jn)

Every one who drinks
of this water
will thirst again,

but whoever drinks
of the water that I shall give him
will never thirst;

the water that I shall give him
will become in him a spring of water
welling up to eternal life.

(Jn)

Why do you discuss the fact that you have no bread?

Do you not yet perceive,
or understand?
Are your hearts hardened?

Having eyes do you not see,
and having ears do you not hear?
And do you not remember?

(Mk)

You seek me

not because you saw signs,
but because you ate your fill of the loaves.

Do not labour for the food which perishes,
but for the food which endures to eternal life,

which the Son of man will give to you;
for on him has God the Father set his seal.

(Jn)

Truly, truly, I say to you,

He who hears my word
and believes him who sent me,
has eternal life;

he does not come into judgement
but has passed from death
to life.

(Jn)

He who eats my flesh
and drinks my blood
abides in me,
and I in him.

(Jn)

Truly, truly, I say to you, if anyone keeps my word, he will never
see death.

(Jn)

This is the bread which came down from heaven,
not such as the fathers ate
and died;
he who eats this bread
will live for ever.

(Jn)

As the living Father sent me,
and I live because of the Father,
so he who eats me
will live because of me.

(Jn)

Truly, truly, I say to you,

it was not Moses who gave you
the bread from heaven;
my Father gives you
the true bread from heaven.

For the bread of God
is that which comes down from heaven
and gives life
to the world.

(Jn)

As Moses lifted up the serpent in the
    wilderness,*
so must the Son of man be lifted up,
that whoever believes in him
may have eternal life.

For God so loved the world
that he gave his only Son,
that whoever believes in him
should not perish
but have eternal life.

(Jn)

No one can come to me unless the Father who sent me draws him;
and I will raise him up at the last day.

(Jn)

A little while,
and you will see me no more;
again a little while,
and you will see me.

(Jn)

Why are you troubled,
and why do questionings arise in your hearts?

*A reference to an ancient story of a talismanic cure for snake bite. A
brass snake was mounted on a pole and sufferers who looked at it were cured.
The 'lifting up' of Jesus on the Cross would be the cure for sufferers from
the bite of the Serpent Satan.

See my hands and my feet,
that it is I myself;

handle me and see;
for a spirit has not flesh and bones
as you see that I have.

(L)

I told you,
and you do not believe.
The works I do in my Father's name,
they bear witness to me;
but you do not believe,
because you do not belong to my sheep.

My sheep hear my voice,
and I know them,
and they follow me;

and I give them eternal life,
and they shall never perish,
and no one shall snatch them
out of my hand.

My Father, who has given them to me,
is greater than all,
and no one is able to snatch them
out of the Father's hand.

I and the Father
are one.

(Jn)

The poem that follows is found in the Revelations to St John in which the writer records an encounter with the Risen Christ on the prison island of Patmos, during which messages are received for seven of the Churches in Asia Minor. At the end of each message, the promise is made 'to him who conquers' (remains faithful to the end). The assembly of these seven promises into one poem is of course arbitrary.

To him who conquers
I will grant to eat of the tree of life,
which is in the paradise of God.

He who conquers
shall not be hurt by the second death.

To him who conquers
I will give some of the hidden manna,
and I will give him a white stone,
with a new name written on the stone
which no one knows
except him who receives it.

He who conquers
and who keeps my works unto the end,
I will give him power over the nations,
and he shall rule them with a rod of iron,
as when earthen pots are broken in pieces,
even as I myself have received power from my Father;
and I will give him the morning star.

He who conquers
shall be clad in white garments,
and I will not blot his name out of the book of life;
I will confess his name before my Father
and before his angels.

He who conquers,
I will make him a pillar in the temple of my God,
never shall he go out of it,
and I will write on him the name of my God,
and the name of the city of my God,
the new Jerusalem which comes down from my God out of
    heaven,
and my own new name.

He who conquers,
I will grant him to sit with me on my throne,
as I myself conquered
and sat down with my Father on his throne.

(Revelation)

12

GOD AND MAN

JESUS defined no doctrines; his teaching, however, provoked a great deal of later doctrinal definition and all the controversy which surrounds that kind of exercise.

God, as Jesus proclaimed Him, is the God revealed in the Old Testament. The whole of the teaching of Jesus is consistent with the theism which he inherited and in which he was brought up. Jesus spoke of God as one who is *known,* and the blasphemy for which he was ultimately arrested and handed over to the Roman authorities to kill (though for their benefit expressed in secular terms) was his insistence on the essential identity between himself and God.

There is much paradox in what Jesus taught, and much that looks at first sight like contradiction. 'I and my Father are one,' he said. And he also said, 'My Father is greater than I.' There is an insistence that God is *Father;* this is the relationship between Jesus and God and also the relationship between mankind and God. The disciples were told to pray: 'Our Father . . .'. The idea of God as Father is an Old Testament one. Peculiar to Jesus, however, is the intense intimacy which uses the diminutive 'Abba'—in everyday English, 'Dad'—to express the relationship. This is very much his own style.

There is much reference to *the Father*; and there is also a great deal of reference to *the Son,* meaning himself. There is also a good deal of reference to *the Spirit* (in Hebrew, *ruach*), which in the Old Testament is found as the instrument of divine action and inspiration. In the Fourth Gospel the Holy Spirit is referred to as *parakletos* or 'Advocate'. Jesus did not define relationships within the divine mystery; he referred to realities beyond any human definition. It was the task of the Church in the three centuries to follow to meet the challenge of heretical groups and seek to define the indefinable, both as to the essential Being of the one God and as to the relationship between the Godhead and the humanity of Jesus. These definitions were necessary human attempts at the impossible in order to safeguard the Truth from distortion by false teachers. Mysteries remain, however, impossible of definition.

Implicit in the teaching of Jesus are two essential truths. The first is the identity between himself and the Father. He came to do the Father's will, he was sent. He came into a human condition which is defined by the Old Testament as having fallen from Grace and being in radical disorder. He entered a humanity out of step both with itself and with God. He came therefore in order to suffer both the tensions and the consequences of the human situation. The conflict was within himself by virtue of the identity he claimed with the Father.

The second truth concerns his identity with the totality of humanity. Jesus did not define a doctrine of man as 'one being with an infinitude of persons'. The Church did that, much later on; but such a doctrine is implicit in the whole of his life and teaching. The two identities, with the Father and with the totality of humanity, represent the mission he came to fulfil.

Using the imagery available to him, Jesus spoke of his *persona* and his mission in nuptial terms, taking their implications for granted. The poetic imagery of marriage which permeates the Old Testament— between Heaven and Earth, between God and man, between God and His Israel, between Christ and his Bride the Church (in New Testament teaching)—pervades the whole of the Gospel, seldom explicit but implicit everywhere.

Jesus defined no doctrines; it was left to others to do that. To one great thinker, St Athanasius, it was left to sum up in a nutshell the whole Christian belief and experience of Jesus:

God became man in order that man might become God!

I thank thee, Father, Lord of heaven and earth,
that thou hast hidden these things
from the wise and understanding
and revealed them
to babes;

yea, Father,
for such was thy gracious will.

All things have been delivered to me by my Father;
and no one knows who the Son is
except the Father,
or who the Father is
except the Son

and any one to whom the Son
chooses to reveal him.

(Q)

Truly, truly, I say to you,

the Son can do nothing of his own accord,
but only what he sees the Father doing;
for whatever he does
that the Son does likewise.

For the Father loves the Son,
and shows him
all that he himself is doing;
and greater works than these
will he show him,
that you may marvel.

For as the Father raises the dead
and gives them life,
so also the Son
gives life to whom he will.

(Jn)

There was a man who had two sons; and the youngest of them said
to his father, 'Father, give me the share of property that falls to me.'
And he divided his living between them. Not many days later, the
younger son gathered all he had and took his journey into a far country,
and there he squandered his property in loose living. And when he
had spent everything, a great famine arose in that country, and he
began to be in want. So he went and joined himself to one of the
citizens of that country, who sent him into his fields to feed swine.
And he would gladly have fed on the pods that the swine ate; and
no one gave him anything.

But when he came to himself he said, 'How many of my father's hired servants have bread enough and to spare, but I perish here with hunger! I will arise and go to my father, and I will say to him, Father, I have sinned against heaven and before you; I am no longer worthy to be called your son; treat me as one of your hired servants.' And he arose and came to his father.

But while he was yet at a distance, his father saw him and had compassion, and ran and embraced him and kissed him. And the son said to him, 'Father, I have sinned against heaven and before you; I am no longer worthy to be called your son.' But the father said to his servants, 'Bring quickly the best robe, and put it on him; and put a ring on his hand, and shoes on his feet; and bring the fatted calf and kill it, and let us eat and make merry; for this my son was lost, and is found.' And they began to make merry.

Now his elder son was in the field; and as he came and drew near to the house, he heard music and dancing. And he called one of the servants and asked what this meant. And he said to him, 'Your brother has come, and your father has killed the fatted calf because he has received him safe and sound.' But he was angry and refused to go in.

His father came out and entreated him, but he answered his father, 'Lo, these many years I have served you, and I never disobeyed your command; Yet you never gave me a kid, that I might make merry with my friends. But when this son of yours came, who has devoured your living with harlots, you killed for him the fatted calf!' And he said to him, 'Son, you are always with me, and all that is mine is yours. It was fitting to make merry and be glad, for this your brother was dead, and is alive; he was lost, and is found.'

(L)

If I am not doing the works of my Father,
then do not believe me;
but if I do them,
even though you do not believe me,
believe the works,

that you may know and understand
that the Father is in me
and I am in the Father.

(Jn)

I shall be with you a little longer,
and then I go to him who sent me;

You will seek me
and you will not find me;
where I am
you cannot come.

(Jn)

If you love me, you will keep my commandments. And I will pray
the Father, and he will give you another Counsellor, to be with you
for ever, even the Spirit of truth, whom the world cannot receive,
because it neither sees him nor knows him; you know him, for he
dwells with you, and will be in you.

(Jn)

In that day you will know

that I
am in my Father
and you
in me,
and I
in you.

(Jn)

He who receives you
receives me,
and he who receives me
receives him who sent me.

(M)

The hour is coming, and now is, when the true worshippers will worship
the Father in spirit and truth, for such the Father seeks to worship
him. God is spirit, and those who worship him must worship in spirit
and truth.

(Jn)

Truly, truly, I say to you,

He who receives any one whom I send
receives me;
and he who receives me
receives him who sent me.

(Jn)

If you had known me,
you would have known my Father also;
henceforth you know him
and have seen him.

(Jn)

Whoever receives one such child in my name
receives me;
and whoever receives me,
receives not me
but him who sent me.

(Mk)

I came from the Father
and have come into the world;
again, I am leaving the world
and going to the Father.

(Jn)

Let not your hearts be troubled,
neither let them be afraid.

You heard me say to you,
'I go away,
'and I will come to you.'

If you loved me, you would have rejoiced,
because I go to the Father;
for the Father is greater than I.

And now I have told you
before it takes place,
so that when it does take place,
you may believe.

(Jn)

If I glorify myself,
my glory is nothing;
it is my Father who glorifies me,
of whom you say that he is your God.

But you have not known him;
I know him.
If I said,
I do not know him,
I should be a liar
like you;

but I do know him
and I keep his word.

(Jn)

But when the Counsellor comes, whom I shall send to you, who
proceeds from the Father, even the Spirit of truth, who proceeds from
the Father, he will bear witness to me.

(Jn)

When the Spirit of truth comes,
he will guide you into all the truth;

for he will not speak
on his own authority,
but whatever he hears
he will speak,

and he will declare to you
the things that are to come.

He will glorify me,
for he will take what is mine
and declare it to you.

All that the Father has is mine;
therefore I said
that he will take what is mine
and declare it to you.

(Jn)

He who has seen me
has seen the Father;

How can you say,
'Show us the Father'?

Do you not believe
that I am in the Father
and the Father in me?

The words that I say to you
I do not speak on my own authority;
but the Father who dwells in me
does his works.

Believe me
that I am in the Father
and the Father in me;

or else believe me
for the sake of the works themselves.

(Jn)

'Saul, Saul, why do you persecute me? . . . I am Jesus, whom you
are persecuting.'*

(Acts)

*The passage that follows is known as the 'High Priestly Prayer' of Jesus,
and is reported in the Fourth Gospel immediately before his arrest in the Garden
of Gethsemane, with the trial, torture, and execution that followed. It is among
other things a proclamation of the relationship which Jesus claims to exist
between the Father, himself and mankind—the mankind of the New Covenant,
the Church, or perhaps of the Kingdom. Many would see in this prayer a
substantial degree of commentary as well as reporting, and it may well have
been composed out of disconnected sayings of Jesus at other times (as no doubt
most of the Discourses were). This is of small consequence, however, as the
Mind of Jesus is faithfully reported, and the tension between the Kingdom
and the World clearly presented.*

*An encounter, by Saul (St Paul) with the Risen Christ. Saul was engaged
in an active and fanatical persecution of the Christian Church in the decade
after the death and Resurrection of Jesus. In this encounter, which resulted
in the conversion of Saul to the Christian Faith, Jesus makes plain the identity
between himself and his followers: 'I am Jesus, whom you are persecuting.'

Father, the hour has come;
glorify thy Son
that the Son
may glorify thee,
since thou hast given him power
over all flesh,
to give eternal life
to all whom thou hast given him.

And this is eternal life,
that they know thee
the only true God
and Jesus Christ
whom thou hast sent.

I glorified thee on earth,
having accomplished the work which thou gavest me to do;
and now, Father,
glorify thou me in thy own presence
with the glory which I had with thee before the world was
 made.

I have manifested thy name
to the men whom thou gavest me
out of the world;
thine they were,
and thou gavest them to me
and they have kept thy word.

Now they know
that everything that thou hast given me
is from thee;
for I have given them the words
which thou gavest me,
and they have received them
and know in truth
that I came from thee;
and they have believed
that thou didst send me.

I am praying for them;
I am not praying for the world
but for those whom thou hast given me,
for they are thine;
all mine are thine,
and thine are mine,
and I am glorified in them.

And now I am no more in the world,
but they are in the world,
and I am coming to thee.

Holy Father,
keep them in thy name,
which thou hast given me,
that they may be one,
even as we are one.

While I was with them,
I kept them in thy name,
which thou hast given me;

I have guarded them,
and none of them is lost
but the son of perdition,
that the scripture might be fulfilled.

But now I am coming to thee;
and these things I speak in the world,
that they may have my joy
fulfilled in themselves.

I have given them thy word;
and the world has hated them
because they are not of the world,
even as I am not of the world.

I do not pray
that thou shouldst take them out of the world,
but that thou shouldst keep them from the evil one.

They are not of the world,
even as I am not of the world.

Sanctify them in the truth;
thy word is truth.
As thou didst send me into the world,
so I have sent them into the world.
And for their sake I consecrate myself,
that they also may be consecrated in truth.

I do not pray for these only,
but for all those
who believe in me through their word,
that they may all be one;
even as thou, Father, art in me,
and I in thee,
that they also may be in us,
so that the world may believe
that thou hast sent me.

The glory which thou hast given to me
I have given to them,
that they may be one
even as we are one,
I in them
and thou in me,
that they may become perfectly one,
so that the world may know
that thou hast sent me
and hast loved them
even as thou hast loved me.

Father,
I desire that they also,
whom thou hast given me,
may be with me where I am,
to behold my glory
which thou hast given me
in thy love for me
before the foundation of the world.

O righteous Father,
the world has not known thee,
but I have known thee;
and these know that thou hast sent me.

I made known to them thy name,*
and I will make it known,
that the love with which thou hast loved me
may be in them,
and I in them.

(Jn)

*In Hebrew thought, the name of anything sums up the whole essence, the whole nature of a thing. Thus making known the Name of God is the revelation of the whole nature of God, the whole of the Divine Personality.

PART 2

From Apocryphal Sources

13

CONCERNING
ESOTERIC KNOWLEDGE

THE New Testament is made up of four types of books. The most numerous, and thus the greater part of the whole, are the letters to various Christian congregations, written by, or attributed to, the Apostles Peter, Paul, John, and Jude, plus the Letter to the Hebrews (probably the Church in Rome) by an unknown author. Most of these are by St Paul and date from the mid-50s to the mid-60s of the first century. The Pauline letters are thus older than the Gospels by quite an appreciable period, though not older than the sources from which the Gospels were compiled. With the Letters and the Gospels comes the book of the Acts of the Apostles, and the visionary (and rather difficult) book known as Revelation.

These writings are a number out of a multitude. There are many other letters from Clement and other early Church leaders of the end of the first century; there are works attributed (doubtfully) to other Apostles; there are narratives, 'acts', of this notable person and that; revelations of various kinds, and not a few gospels or fragments of gospels.

There is, as we have seen, a *canon* of writings which the Church has come to regard as Scriptural; authoritative, reliable, truthful, and in some manner inspired both in content and in editorship. (It is easy to overlook the possibility of inspirational editing and compilation.) There is not an equivalent *corpus* of apocryphal material; it proliferates, and trails off, fuzzy round the edges, not infrequently confused, diluted, or patently corrupted by fads and fancies. There has thus been a tendency, for many centuries, to look askance at the whole field and suspect, as it were under every bed, the dark influence of *Gnosticism*.

The word *gnosis* is, quite simply, the Greek for 'knowledge'. It is used in the religious and philosophical context to refer to *esoteric knowledge*. As Victor White explains:

A gnostic, then, is a Knowing One; one who knows, or claims to know, things unknown (= unconscious) to the generality of men . . . the *gnosis* which we find in gnosticism stands in striking contrast to that sort of 'knowledge' which had been sought by classical Greek philosophy and science:

nay further, the success of gnosticism would seem to be largely due to the intellectual bankruptcy and scepticism—the distrust both of the senses and of the reason—which had been produced by the later phases of Greek intellectualist thought . . . To the Golden Age of Greek inquiry and speculation succeeded that amorphous movement which we call Hellenism; to its search for clarity succeeded a search for mystery and a love of mystification; to its confidence in reason, a distrust of, if not a contempt for, reason, and a hankering for some sort of revelation; to its optimistic view of an ordered cosmos, a profound sense of chaos and misery of the material world; to the classical cult of the human body, a contempt for the body and for all bodily manifestations; to the philosopher's attempt to overcome and transmute phantasy and myth into exact logical concepts and scientific thought, a reversion to myth, or rather the importation and adaptation of foreign myths and the formation of new myths. The philosophers themselves had perhaps contributed much to their own undoing.[1]

Gnosticism is therefore more of an ambience than a religion. Gnostic cults of all kinds proliferated. Here it may be said that there is nothing necessarily the matter with *gnosis* as such. Intuitive awareness at many levels is part of the natural human make-up, and a great deal of the stuff of gnosticism is to be found in depth psychology. Few people have done more to rehabilitate the very stuff of *gnosis* than C. G. Jung, and perhaps as distinguished a modern gnostic as may be met with is the remarkable Rudolf Steiner. But Victor White reminds us that,

at this point it becomes necessary to introduce a distinction between *Gnosis* and a *Gnostic* on the one hand, and *Gnosticism* and what we may call a *Gnosticist* on the other. By the latter I would understand one who, in addition to being a gnostic, makes an 'ism' of his gnosis. The distinction is of importance, if only because it is a profound mistake to suppose that, in rejecting gnosticism, the main body of the Christian Church thereby rejected gnosis or could find no room for the gnostic. It neither did—nor could. The revelation which the Church herself accepted, and which gave her very *raison d'être*, was itself in its origins a gnosis..[2]

The caution which attends the Christian when approaching apocryphal material derives from a not uncommon distortion of original sources in favour of a particular sectarian viewpoint. Of the apocryphal Gospel of Thomas, Grant and Freedman claim that 'it is probably our most significant witness to the early perversion of Christianity by those who

[1] Victor White, OP, *God and the Unconscious* (Fontana, 1960), p. 207.
[2] ibid., p. 209.

wanted to create Jesus in their own image. Thus it stands, like Lot's wife, as a new but permanently valuable witness to men's desire to make God's revelation serve them. Ultimately it testifies not to what Jesus said but to what men wished he had said.'[3]

This *caveat* is worth entering because we shall encounter a good deal of this gospel later on, but in the main it is the evidence of perversion by special pleading, or by 'doctoring' of the text in favour of a sectarian viewpoint that has, until recently, consigned apocryphal material to a kind of limbo. Other reservations abound, but they concern imprecision, confused presentation, and the generally second- or third-rate nature of much of the material. However, there are signs of a renewed interest in the apocryphal gospels among New Testament scholars as it is possible that they may help us to trace more clearly the way in which the canonical Gospels reached their present form, and shed more light than was supposed upon the general ambience of the early New Testament period. Of another apocryphal gospel fragment, Ron Cameron states: 'Most of all, the discovery of the *Secret Gospel of Mark* has made us privy to new and unparalleled information about the various editions of the Gospel of Mark, and has brought to our attention the widespsread esoteric tradition among the earliest believers in Jesus.'[4] The problems faced by the early Fathers of the Church, in countering the enthusiasms of the unbalanced esotericist, are stated in one of the letters of Clement to Theodore: 'You did well in silencing the unspeakable teachings of the Carpocratians [a gnostic sect who taught a mixture of sexual licence and popular esotericism]. Now of the things they keep saying about the divinely inspired Gospel according to Mark, some are altogether falsifications and others, even if they do contain some true elements, nevertheless are not reported truly. For the true things being mixed with inventions, are falsified, so that, as the saying goes, even the salt loses its savour.'[5]

In preparing an anthology of the reported sayings of Jesus from apocryphal sources, therefore, it must be emphasized that *everything* has to be treated with caution. It must also be remembered that not all scholars are agreed on the degree of caution, and in this connection it will be worth our while to return to the Gospel of Thomas to discover something of the diversity of opinion and approach between scholars some twenty-five years apart.

[3] Grant and Freedman, *The Secret Sayings of Jesus* (Fontana, 1960), p. 16.
[4] Ron Cameron, *The Other Gospels* (Lutterworth, 1983), p. 68.
[5] ibid., p. 69.

Grant and Freedman, in their translation and commentary *The Secret Sayings of Jesus*, quite firmly present the Gospel of Thomas as a Gnostic compilation which gives support to the Gnostic tendency to see mankind as divided between the 'spiritual', the 'psychic', and the 'material'. There are 'three kinds of Churches': that of the *elect,* that of the *called,* and that of the *captive.* The four canonical Gospels contain the 'psychic teaching' of Jesus, but of course only the 'elect' were competent to interpret them. Behind this hierarchical understanding lurks a tendency to reject material creation as evil, and common to many gnostic groups was the notion that sexual intercourse was absolutely evil. Man's true goal is to reach a state such as obtained before the Fall; the New Creation is sexless. As the primal being is called Man, it follows that all human beings must become men! 'What we find in this Gnostic system is a complete spiritualisation of the Christian gospel. The spiritualisation is accompanied by a love of the esoteric and a love of finding the esoteric where it might not seem to be present . . . *as a whole* Thomas must be considered a Gnostic Gospel.'[6]

There is a considerable overlap between Thomas and both Matthew and Luke (in particular the 'Q' material), but the treatment is quite different: 'Even within the Sermon on the Mount, [Thomas] omits everything that has to do with moral conduct and the performance of good works. He is not concerned with what Christians do but with what they know.'[7]

In addition it can be said that a twentieth-century successor of the Gnostics might well find much of the Gospel of Thomas attractive. Thomas is silent about sin and forgiveness. He records no miracles or, indeed, deeds of Jesus. There are no embarrassing stories about demons and the exorcism of demons. The kingdom of God is almost entirely inward, unrelated to time or history. One need not love his enemies. In fact there is practically nothing which a disciple need do.[8]

Grant and Freedman date the Gospel of Thomas no earlier than the middle of the second century and, while thinking it possible that an earlier and more 'orthodox' version than the Coptic text may have existed, regard differences between Thomas and Matthew/Luke as evidence of 'garbling' or manipulation by Thomas. Their book was published in Great Britain in 1960.

[6] Grant and Freedman, op. cit., pp. 83-5.
[7] ibid., p. 102.
[8] ibid., p. 108.

Another American scholar, Ron Cameron, in his book *The Other Gospels* (1983) differs very substantially from Grant and Freedman. As to the date of composition, he asserts: 'Its earliest possible date of composition would be in the middle of the first century, when other sayings collections began to be compiled . . . the most likely date of its composition would be in the second half of the first century, almost certainly in Syria.'[9] Cameron belongs to a school of New Testament scholarship which would date the canonical Gospels at about the middle of the second century. Thomas is thus presented as an earlier composition. And in marked contrast to Grant and Freedman he claims that,

Most of the sayings in the Gospel of Thomas have parallels in the 'synoptic' gospels of Matthew, Mark, and Luke in the New Testament. Analysis of each of these sayings reveals that the sayings in the Gospel of Thomas are either preserved in forms more primitive than those in the parallel sayings in the New Testament or are developments of more primitive forms of such sayings . . . this suggests that the Gospel of Thomas is based on a tradition of sayings which is closely related to that of the canonical gospels but which has experienced a separate process of transmission.[10]

It is clear that scholarship, in respect of the apocryphal books, is far from unanimous. Cameron gives none of the warnings that Grant and Freedman utter. The Gospel of Thomas presents its material as 'the secret sayings which the living Jesus spoke [i.e. the Risen Christ?] and which Didymos Judas Thomas wrote down. And he said, "Whoever finds the interpretation of these sayings will not experience death." ' Cameron claims that 'the discernment of the meaning of these sayings of Jesus was believed to bring secret wisdom. These sayings were understood as the voice of divine Wisdom revealing herself. Their interpretation is crucial; recognizing their meaning, a matter of life and death. Fundamentally therefore, the Gospel of Thomas is an esoteric book which, according to the catechetical instruction imparted in Saying 50, reveals one's origin ("the light"), identity ("elect", "children"), and destiny ("repose").'[11]

The Gospel of Thomas is but one apocryphal gospel, albeit the most complete and probably the most interesting. It is clear that we are in a very different ambience than we were with the four canonical

[9] Cameron, op. cit., pp. 24-5.
[10] ibid., p. 24.
[11] ibid.

Gospels. There is some material that it is very much worth our while gleaning from the New Testament Apocrypha, but it is clear that it must be approached with a good deal of caution.

14

THE TEXTS

FOR all that there exists a large number of apocryphal writings, the choice for an anthology such as this is limited. I have therefore drawn upon three sources with a single quotation from a fourth, concluding with something of a flourish with an extract from a fifth. These are as follows:

(i) The *Gospel of Thomas* (T) has already been outlined. The complete text was first uncovered, having been lost for centuries, in 1945 at Nag Hammadi in Egypt and the Coptic text first published in 1959. It was therefore something of a novelty when Grant and Freedman wrote their book. Like the other apocryphal books it has no accepted chapter and verse numbering and is essentially a collection of 'sayings' such as, perhaps, the supposed 'Q' might have been. There is a suggestion that it is presented as a post-resurrection teaching of Jesus, but this is not necessarily so and would have been merely a literary device. The translation I have used is that of Thomas O. Lambdin (*The Nag Hammadi Library*) and is reproduced in *The Other Gospels* by Ron Cameron. I have used the translations given in this work in every case.

(ii) The *Apocryphon of James* (AJ), also discovered in 1945, presents sayings of Jesus as a dialogue between the Risen Christ and the disciples Peter and James the Just, brother of the Lord. There is no narrative structure and the dialogue presentation soon fades away. Cameron, whose own translation I use, suggests a date between the middle of the first century and the end of the second. It was used to combat the arguments of heretical groups and it resembles the Fourth Gospel in its combination of individual sayings to make up both dialogue and 'farewell discourses'.

(iii) The *Epistula Apostolorum* (EA), discovered in 1895 and published in 1919, dates from a little later than the canonical Gospels, perhaps from the second half of the second century and is a deliberate credal statement of the orthodox, catholic belief as opposed to the teachings of the gnostic sects. It gives a broad résumé of the life and ministry of Jesus and incorporates some sayings which are presented as post-resurrection teachings of considerable interest. There is nothing doctrinally suspect about this work though two versions, one in Coptic and the other in Ethiopic, differ substantially in detail, the Coptic text being the more reliable, though incomplete. The translation is by Hugo Duensing and Richard E. Taylor (*New Testament Aprocrypha*).

(iv) One quotation from the now fragmentary *Gospel of the Hebrews* (GH) comes via St Jerome who quotes it in his *Commentary on Ephesians, Chapter 3* (translation by Philipp Vielhauer and George Ogg, *New Testament Apocrypha*).

(v) The 'tailpiece' is a very ancient hymn, presented as having been sung by Jesus and his Apostles in a kind of liturgical dance at the conclusion of the Last Supper. It is found in 'John's Preaching of the Gospel' in the Acts of John, a document which is probably contemporary with the Fourth Gospel, possibly connected in some way with the 'Johannine School', but exhibiting both gnostic and docetic tendencies in places. The translation used is by Knut Schäferdiek and G. C. Stead (*New Testament Apocrypha*).

The arrangement of the material

The choice of material is, inevitably, arbitrary. I have avoided too much obvious repetition of material already presented in the first part of this anthology. I have also avoided sayings which seem to me to be somehow 'out of character' in their apparent overbalance towards, for example, the extreme gnostic idea that women must become men in order to be saved. The underlying theme, that of men and women in the resurrection being 'as the angels in heaven' and 'neither marrying nor being given in marriage', is preserved in other texts which are included.

It would not be difficult to reproduce the ten main headings of the first part of this anthology and arrange the material in this way. There is, however, a shortage of suitable material and so I have assembled it under three headings: *The Kingdom, Dedication,* and *Wholeness.* The final hymn is presented as an *envoi* to the whole work.

The presentation of the material

The translations I have used were presented in prose form, which is the normal manner of biblical presentation. I have arranged most of them in verse form as was suggested to me by my own reading, and thus the presentation is much the same as in the first part of this anthology. I have removed numerous scholarly comments within the text—alternative readings, brackets, and so forth—and where necessary I have altered spelling from American to English forms.

15

THE KINGDOM

THE material which follows is unfamiliar to all but a handful of general readers but fits into and complements the teaching concerning the Kingdom and Eternal Life in the canonical Gospels. The material from the Apocryphon of James reveals, both in this section and in those that follow, an astringency which, though by no means lacking in the New Testament, is somewhat startling. The whole work portrays a Jesus who combines reassurance with energetic and outspoken requirements for renewed dedication and urgency.

*

[The kingdom] will not come by waiting for it.
It will not be a matter of saying
'Here it is'
or 'There it is.'
Rather,
the kingdom of the Father
is spread out upon the earth,
and men do not see it.

(T)

O you wretched!
O you unfortunates!
O you dissemblers of the truth!
O you falsifiers of knowledge!
O you sinners against the spirit!

Do you even now dare to listen,
when it behoved you to speak from the beginning?
Do you even now dare to sleep,
when it behoved you to be awake from the beginning,
in order that the kingdom of heaven might receive you?

In truth, I say to you,

it is easier for a holy one to sink into defilement,
and for a man of light to sink into darkness,
than for you to reign—
or not to reign.

(AJ)

Truly I say to you,

none will be saved
unless they believe in my cross.
But those who have believed in my cross,
theirs is the kingdom of God.

Therefore,
become seekers for death,
just as the dead who seek for life,
for that which they seek is revealed to them.
And what is there to concern them?

When you turn yourselves towards death,
it will make known to you election.

(AJ)

If you do not fast as regards the world,
you will not find the kingdom.
If you do not observe the sabbath as a sabbath,
you will not see the Father.

(T)

In truth I say to you,

none of those who are afraid of death
will be saved.

For the kingdom of God belongs
to those who have put themselves to death.

(AJ)

If those who lead you, say to you,
'See, the kingdom is in the sky,'
then the birds of the sky will precede you.
If they say to you,
'it is in the sea,'
then the fish will precede you.

Rather,
the kingdom is inside of you,
and it is outside of you.

When you come to know yourselves,
then you will become known,
and you will realize that it is you
who are the sons of the living Father.

But if you will not know yourselves,
you dwell in poverty,
and it is you who are that poverty.

(T)

Let not the kingdom of heaven become desolate among you. Do not become arrogant on account of the light which illumines. Rather, become to yourselves in this manner, as I am to you. For you I have placed myself under the curse, in order that you may be saved.

(AJ)

Woe to you who are in need of an advocate!
Woe to you who are in need of grace!
Blessed are those who have spoken freely
and have produced grace for yourselves.

Make yourselves like strangers;
of what sort are they in the estimation of your city?
Why are you troubled
when you oust yourselves of your own accord
and depart from your city?
Why do you abandon your dwelling place of your own
    accord,
readying it for those who desire to dwell in it?
O you exiles and fugitives!
Woe to you, because you will be caught!

Or perhaps you imagine that the Father is a lover of
  humanity?
Or that he is persuaded by prayers?
Or that he is gracious to one on behalf of another?
Or that he bears with one who seeks?

For he knows the desire
and also that which the flesh needs.
Because it is not [the flesh] which yearns for the soul.
For without the soul the body does not sin,
just as the soul is not saved without the spirit.

But if the soul is saved when it is without evil,
and if the spirit also is saved,
then the body becomes sinless.
For it is the spirit which animates the soul,
but it is the body which kills it—
that is, it is [the soul] which kills itself.

Truly I say to you,

[the Father] will not forgive the sin of the soul at all,
nor the guilt of the flesh.
For none of those who have worn the flesh will be
  saved.

For do you imagine
that many have found the kingdom of heaven?
Blessed is the one
who has seen himself as the fourth one in Heaven.

(AJ)

He who is near me
is near the fire,
and he who is far from me
is far from the kingdom.

(T)

Become zealous about the Word.
For the Word's first condition is faith;
the second is love;
the third is works.

Now from these comes life.
For the Word is like a grain of wheat.
When some one sowed it,
he believed in it;
and when it sprouted,
he loved it,
because he looked forward to many grains in the place of
    one;
and when he worked it,
he was saved,
because he prepared it for food.
Again he left some grains to sow.

Thus it is also possible
for you to receive the kingdom of heaven;
unless you receive it through knowledge,
you will not be able to find it.

(AJ)

Truly I say to you,

no one ever will enter the kingdom of heaven
if I bid him,
but rather
because you yourselves are full.

(AJ)

The kingdom of the Father is like a certain man who wanted to kill
a powerful man. In his own house he drew his sword and stuck it
into the wall in order to find out whether his hand could carry through.
Then he slew the powerful man.

(T)

Those here who do the will of my Father
are my brothers and my mother.
It is they who will enter
the kingdom of my Father.

(T)

For the kingdom of heaven is like an ear of grain which sprouted in a field. And when it ripened it scattered its fruit and, in turn, filled the field with ears of grain for another year. You also: be zealous to reap for yourselves an ear of life, in order that you may be filled with the kingdom.

(AJ)

Truly I say to you, all who have believed in me and who will believe in him who sent me I will lead up to heaven, to the place which my Father has prepared for the elect, and I will give you the chosen kingdom in rest, and eternal life.

(EA)

Blessed are the solitary and elect,
for you will find the kingdom.
For you are from it,
and to it you will return.

(T)

16

DEDICATION

NEITHER in the canonical, nor in the apocryphal books does Jesus do any man's thinking for him. Poetry, poetic exaggeration and parable are mixed with astringent exhortation and sometimes outright rebuke. The Gospel is a matter of life or death and a sense of urgency pervades everything Jesus says or does.

The themes are the same: man must seek maturity, he must become responsible. A man is responsible and will be held responsible; he must rise to his responsibilities, which include spreading the Good News, furthering the kingdom. The rewards of dedication are incalculable, but man is weak, a sinner.

I took my place in the midst of the world,
and I appeared to them in flesh.
I found all of them intoxicated;
I found none of them thirsty.
And my soul became afflicted for the sons of men,
because they are blind in their hearts
and do not have sight;
for empty they came into the world,
and empty too they seek to leave the world.
But for the moment they are intoxicated.
When they shake off their wine,
then they will repent.

(T)

As long as I am with you,
give heed to me and obey me.
But when I am to depart from you,
remember me.

And remember me
because I was with you
without your knowing me.

Blessed are those who have known me.
Woe to those who have heard
and have not believed!
Blessed are those who have not seen
but have had faith.

(AJ)

It is impossible
for a man to mount two horses
or to stretch two bows.

And it is impossible
for a servant to serve two masters;
otherwise, he will honour the one
and treat the other contemptuously.

No man drinks old wine
and immediately desires to drink new wine.
And new wine
is not put into old wineskins,
lest they burst;
nor is old wine
put into a new wineskin,
lest it spoil it.

An old patch
is not sewn into a new garment,
because a tear would result.

(T)

Be zealous to be saved without being urged. Rather, be ready on your
own and, if possible, go before me. For thus the Father will love you.

(AJ)

I am not your master.

Because you have drunk,
you have become intoxicated
from the bubbling spring
which I have measured out.

(T)

Have you discovered, then,
the beginning
that you look for the end?
For where the beginning is,
there will the end be.

Blessed is he
who will take his place in the beginning:
he will know the end
and will not experience death.

(T)

But if someone believes in me and does not do my commandments,
although he has acknowledged my name he receives no benefit from
it and has run a futile course. For such will be in error and in ruin,
since they have disregarded my commandments.

(EA)

Whoever believes that the All itself is deficient
is himself completely deficient.

(T)

Whoever has ears,
let him hear.
There is light
within a man of light,
and he lights up the whole world.
If he does not shine,
he is darkness.

(T)

Do you not desire, then, to be filled?
And is your heart drunk?
Do you not desire, then, to be sober?
Therefore, be ashamed!

And now, waking or sleeping,
remember that you have seen the Son of Man,
and with him you have spoken,
and to him you have listened.

Woe to those who have seen the Son of Man.
Blessed are those who have not seen the Man,
and who have not consorted with him,
and who have not spoken with him,
and who have not listened to anything from him.
Yours is life!

Know, therefore,
that he healed you when you were ill,
in order that you might reign.

Woe to those who have rested from their illness,
because they will relapse again into illness!
Blessed are those who have not been ill,
and have known rest before they became ill.
Yours is the kingdom of God!

Therefore I say to you,

become full
and leave no place within you empty,
since the Coming One is able to mock you.

(AJ)

Many are standing at the door,
but it is the solitary
who will enter the bridal chamber.

(T)

Therefore,
obey me, my brothers.
Understand what the great light is.
The Father does not need me.
For a father does not need a son,
but it is a son who needs the father.
To him I am going,
for the Father of the Son is not in need of you.

(AJ)

That which you have will save you
if you bring it forth from yourselves.
That which you do not have within you
will kill you if you do not have it within you.

(T)

What is merit when you do the will of the Father if it is not given
you as a gift, while are tempted by Satan? But if you are oppressed
by Satan and are persecuted and you do [the Father's] will, I say that
he will love you and will make you equal with me and will consider
that you have become beloved through his providence according to
your free choice.

(AJ)

Blessed is the lion which becomes man
when consumed by man;
and cursed is the man
whom the lion consumes,
and the lion becomes man.*

(T)

Therefore I say to you

become full,
in order that you may not be diminished.

*The lion is a symbol of the sexual drive.

Those who are diminished, however,
will not be saved.
For fullness is good
and diminution is bad.

Therefore,

just as it is good for you to be diminished
and, on the other hand,
bad for you to be filled,
so also
the one who is full is diminished;
and the one who is diminished is not filled
as the one who is diminished is filled,
and the one who is full, for his part,
brings his sufficiency to completion.

Therefore,

it is fitting to be diminished
while you can still be filled,
and to be filled
while it is still possible to be diminished,
in order that you can fill yourselves the more.

Therefore,

become full of the spirit
but be diminished of reason.
For reason is of the soul;
and it is soul.

(AJ)

Woe to the flesh that depends on the soul;
woe to the soul that depends on the flesh.

(T)

Truly, I say to you,

Whoever will hear you
and believe in me,
he will receive from you
the light of the seal through me
and baptism through me;
you will become fathers
and servants
and also masters.

(EA)

O Lord, there are many round the drinking trough, but there is nothing in the cistern.

(T)

I have cast fire upon the world,
and see,
I am guarding it until it blazes.

(T)

Become haters of hypocrisy and evil thought. For it is thought which gives birth to hypocrisy, but hypocrisy is far from the truth.

(AJ)

No prophet is accepted in his own village;
no physician heals those who know him.

(T)

Whoever finds the world and becomes rich, let him renounce the world.

(T)

Become passers-by.

(T)

If [circumcision] were beneficial,
their father would beget them
already circumcised from their mother.
Rather,
the true circumcision in spirit
has become completely profitable.

(T)

Blessed are they who have been persecuted within themselves.
It is they who have truly come to know the Father.
Blessed are the hungry,
for the belly of him who desires shall be filled.

(T)

Truly I say to you,

you will first of all be called fathers,
for you will have revealed to them
with seemly hearts and in love
the things of the kingdom of heaven.

And you will be called servants,
for they will receive by my hand
through you
the baptism of life
and the forgiveness of their sins.

And you will be called masters,
for you have given them the word
without grudging
and have warned them;
and when you warned them
they turned back.

(EA)

Blessed is he
who came into being
before he came into being.

If you become my disciples
and listen to my words,
these stones will minister to you.

For there are five trees in Paradise
which remain undisturbed
summer and winter
and whose leaves do not fall.

Whoever becomes acquainted with them
will not experience death.

(T)

Let him who seeks
continue seeking
until he finds.

When he finds,
he will become troubled.

When he becomes troubled,
he will be astonished,

and then he will rule over the All.

(T)

Whoever finds the interpretation of these sayings will not experience
death.

(T)

WHOLENESS

WHOLENESS is integration; man's integration within himself and with himself at every level; man's integration with his fellow men, and with creation; man's integration with God. Not a return to primal innocence, but a calling forward and upward into the new heaven and the new earth. Integration is the keynote of the kingdom. As it is written in Revelation: 'There shall be a new heaven and a new earth', and, 'Behold, I make all things new.'

Behold,
I shall depart from you.
I am going
and I do not desire to remain with you any longer—
just as you yourselves have not desired.
Now, then, follow me quickly.

Therefore I say to you,

for your sake I have descended.
You are the beloved;
you are those
who will become a cause of life for many.

Beseech the Father.
Implore God often,
and he will give to you.

Blessed is the one who has seen you with him
when he is proclaimed among the angels
and glorified among the saints.

Yours is life!
Rejoice and be glad as children of God.
Keep his will
in order that you may be saved.
Take reproof from me
and save yourselves.

I intercede on your behalf
with the Father,
and he will forgive you much.

(AJ)

When you see your likeness,
you rejoice.
But when you see your images
which came into being before you,
and which neither die nor become manifest,
how much you will have to bear!

(T)

This heaven will pass away,
and the one above it will pass away.
The dead are not alive,
and the living will not die.
In the days when you consumed what is dead,
you made it what is alive.
When you come to dwell in the light,
what will you do?
On the day when you were one
you became two.
But when you become two,
what will you do?

(T)

Recognize what is in your sight,
and that which is hidden from you will become plain to you.
For there is nothing hidden
which will not become manifest.

(T)

When you make the two one,
and when you make the inside like the outside
and the outside like the inside,
and the above like the below,

and when you make the male and the female
one and the same,
so that the male be not male
nor the female female;

and when you fashion eyes in place of an eye,
and a hand in place of a hand,
and a foot in place of a foot,
and a likeness in place of a likeness;
then will you enter the kingdom.

(T)

Truly, I say to you,

I will come as does the sun that shines,
and shining seven times brighter
than it is in my brightness;
with the wings of the clouds
carrying me in splendour
and the sign of the cross before me,
I will come down to earth
to judge the living and the dead.

(EA)

When you make the two one,
you will become the sons of man,
and when you say,
'Mountain, move away,'
it will move away.

(T)

Truly, I say to you,

as my Father awakened me from the dead,
in the same manner you also will arise

and be taken up above the heavens
to the place of which I have spoken to you
from the beginning,
to the place which he who sent me
has prepared for you.

And thus will I complete
all arrangements for salvation:

being unbegotten
and yet begotten of man,
being without flesh
and yet I have worn flesh,
for on that account have I come,
that you [obtain the resurrection in your flesh,
a garment that will not pass away.]*

(EA)

If they say to you,
'Where did you come from?'
say to them,
'We came from the light,
'the place where light came into being
'of its own accord
'and established itself
'and became manifested through their image.'

If they say to you,
'Is it you?'
say,
'We are its children,
'and we are the elect of the Living Father.'

If they ask you,
'What is the sign of your Father in you?'
say to them,
'it is movement and repose.'

(T)

*Words in brackets taken from the Ethiopic text, the Coptic having lines missing at this point.

When you see the one who was not born of woman,
prostrate yourselves on your faces
and worship him.
That one is your Father.

(T)

I am he who exists from the Undivided.
I was given some of the things of my Father.

(T)

On that account I have descended to the place of Lazarus, and have
preached to the righteous and to the prophets, that they may come
forth from the rest which is below and go up to what is above.

(EA)

It is I who am the light
which is above them all.
It is I who am the All.

From me did the All come forth,
and unto me did the All extend.

Split a piece of wood,
and I am there.
Lift up the stone,
and you will find me there.

(T)

The images are manifest to man,
but the light in them remains concealed
in the image of the light of the Father.
He will become manifest,
but his image will remain concealed by his light.

(T)

I shall give you
what no eye has seen
and what no ear has heard
and what no hand has touched
and what has never occurred to the human mind.

(T)

When you disrobe without being ashamed
and take up your garments
and place them under your feet
like little children
and tread on them,
then you will see the Son of the Living One,
and you will not be afraid.

(T)

If the flesh came into being because of spirit,
it is a wonder.
But if spirit came into being because of the body,
it is a wonder of wonders.
Indeed, I am amazed
at how this great wealth
has made its home in this poverty.

(T)

Rise up,
and I will reveal to you
what is above heaven
and what is in heaven,
and your rest that is in the kingdom of heaven.

For my Father has given me the power
to take you up
and those who believe in me.

(EA)

Love your brother like your soul,
guard him like the pupil of your eye.

(T)

And never be joyful,
save when ye behold your brother with love.

(GH)

On that day, when I took the form of the angel Gabriel, I appeared to Mary and spoke with her. Her heart received me and she believed; I formed myself and entered into her womb; I became flesh, for I alone was servant to myself with respect to Mary in an appearance of the form of an angel. So will I do, after I have gone to the Father.

(EA)

When the hundredth part
and the twentieth part
is completed,
between Pentecost
and the feast of unleavened bread,
will the coming of the Father take place.

(EA)

I am wholly in my Father
and my Father is in me.

(EA)

Truly, I say to you, the resurrection of the flesh will happen while the soul and the spirit are in it.

(EA)

He who has recognized the world
has found the body,
but he who has found the body
is superior to the world.

(T)

The heavens and the earth will be rolled up in your presence. And the one who lives from the Living One will not see death . . . Whoever finds himself is superior to the world.

(T)

But it happened, as I was about to come down from the Father of all, I passed by the Heavens; I put on the wisdom of the Father and the power of his might. I was in the heavens, and I passed by the angels and archangels in their form, as if I were one of them among the dominions and powers. I passed through them, possessing the wisdom of him who sent me. But the chief leader of the angels is Michael, and Gabriel and Uriel and Raphael, but they followed me to the fifth firmament, thinking in their hearts that I was one of them. But the Father gave me power of this nature.

And in that day I adorned the archangels with a wondrous voice that they might go up to the altar of the Father and serve and complete the service until I should go to him. Thus I did it through the wisdom of the likeness. For I became all things in everything that I might [   ] the plan of the Father and perfect the glory of him who sent me, and might go to him.

(EA)

What you look forward to has already come, but you do not recognize it.

(T)

THE HYMN OF JESUS

THE ecstatic dance has long been a part of the Jewish religious tradition and ecstatics have always featured in Israel. There need be nothing odd about the idea of the Last Supper ending in a dance, despite the almost board-room solemnity that Western Christians have invested it with. St Matthew's Gospel tells us that, 'When they had sung a hymn, they went out to the Mount of Olives.' Here, we are invited to believe, is that hymn!

St John, as reported in The Acts of John, tells us that Jesus said: ' "Before I am delivered to them, let us sing a hymn to the Father, and so go to meet what lies before us." So he told us to form a circle, holding one another's hands, and himself stood in the middle and said, "Answer Amen to me" ' So Jesus began to sing the hymn and to say:

Glory be to thee, Father.

[And we circled round him and answered him,] *Amen.*

Glory be to thee, Logos:
Glory be to thee, Grace.   *Amen.*

Glory be to thee, Spirit:
Glory be to thee, Holy One:
Glory be to thy Glory.   *Amen.*

We praise thee, Father:
We thank thee, Light:
In whom darkness dwelleth not.   *Amen.*

And why we give thanks, I tell you:
I will be saved,
And I will save.   *Amen.*

I will be loosed,
And I will loose.   *Amen.*

I will be wounded,
And I will wound.   *Amen.*

I will be born,
And I will bear.   *Amen.*

I will eat,
And I will be eaten. *Amen.*

I will hear,
And I will be heard. *Amen.*

I will be thought,
Being wholly thought. *Amen.*

I will be washed,
And I will wash. *Amen.*

[Grace dances.]

I will pipe,
Dance, all of you. *Amen.*

I will mourn,
Beat you all your breasts. *Amen.*

The one Ogdoad*
Sings praises with us. *Amen.*

The twelfth number**
Dances on high. *Amen.*

To the Universe
Belongs the dancer. *Amen.*

He who does not dance
Does not know what happens. *Amen.*

I will flee
And I will remain. *Amen.*

I will adorn,
And I will be adorned. *Amen.*

I will be united,
And I will unite. *Amen.*

I have no house,
And I have houses. *Amen.*

I have no place,
And I have places. *Amen.*

I have no temple,
And I have temples *Amen.*

*Ogdoad—probably the Heavenly Spheres; Sun, Moon and Planets.
**Twelfth Number—probably the archetypes, the Patriarchs of the Twelve Tribes of Israel.

I am a lamp to you
Who see me.   *Amen.*

I am a mirror to you
Who know me.   *Amen.*

I am a door to you
Who knock on me.   *Amen.*

I am a way to you
The traveller.   *Amen.*

Now if you follow
My dance,

See yourself

In me who am speaking,

And when you have seen what I do,
Keep silence about my mysteries.

You who dance, consider
What I do, for yours is

This passion of Man
Which I am to suffer.

For you could by no means
Have understood what you suffer

Unless to you as Logos
I had been sent by the Father.

You who saw what I suffer
Saw me as suffering yourself,

And seeing it you did not stay
But were wholly moved.

Being moved towards wisdom
You have me as a support:
Rest in me.

Who I am, you shall know
When I go forth.

What I now am seen to be,
That I am not;

What I am you shall see
When you come yourself.

If you knew how to suffer
You would not be able to suffer.

Learn how to suffer
And you shall not be able to suffer.

What you do not know
I myself will teach you.

I am your God,
Not the God of the traitor.

I will that there be prepared
Holy souls for me.

Understand the word
Of wisdom!

As for me,
If you would understand what I was:

By the Word I mocked at all things
And I was not mocked at all.

I exulted:
But do you understand the whole,

And when you have understood it, say,
Glory be to thee, Father.

Say again with me,

Glory be to thee, Father,
Glory be to thee, Word,
Glory be to thee, Holy Spirit.   *Amen.*

[After the Lord had so danced with us, my beloved, he went out. And we were like men amazed or fast asleep, and we fled this way and that.]

(Acts of John)